Egyptology Today

No. 4

1980

THE TOMB OF THE VIZIER RĒʿ-WER AT SAQQARA

SAID EL-FIKEY

OXBOW | books
Oxford & Philadelphia

To Sanaa

This edition published in the United Kingdom in 2024 by
OXBOW BOOKS
81 St Clements, Oxford OX4 1AW

and in the United States by
OXBOW BOOKS
1950 Lawrence Road, Havertown, PA 19083

Paperback Edition: ISBN 979-8-88857-089-0
Digital Edition: ISBN 979-8-88857-090-6 (epub)

First published in 1980 by Aris & Phillips Ltd

Oxbow Books is grateful to the Petrie Museum for their collaboration in bringing out these new editions

Printed in the United Kingdom by CMP Digital Print Solutions

For a complete list of Oxbow titles, please contact:

UNITED KINGDOM
Oxbow Books
Telephone (0)1226 734350
Email: oxbow@oxbowbooks.com
www.oxbowbooks.com

UNITED STATES OF AMERICA
Oxbow Books
Telephone (610) 853-9131, Fax (610) 853-9146
Email: queries@casemateacademic.com
www.casemateacademic.com/oxbow

Oxbow Books is part of the Casemate Group

Front cover: East Wall of the tomb, offering-bearers and butchers at work (see Pl. 11)

CONTENTS

PREFACE

Since 1974, when I started work at Saqqara, I found it was necessary to re-excavate the tomb of Rēʿ-wer, at the south-east corner of the Mortuary Temple of King Teti; for this was one of the Old Kingdom tombs which had originally been excavated by C.M. Firth, between 1920-1923, and recorded by Battiscombe Gunn, and covered with sand and debris since that time.

I am grateful to the Department of Antiquities of the Egyptian Government which financed the excavations. I would like to thank my colleagues, the Chief Inspectors and Inspectors at Saqqara between 1975-1978, especially Dr. Ali El-Khouli, who gave me constant help, and Hassab Allah Tayyib, the photographer at Saqqara.

Throughout the work on this book, I enjoyed the help of my colleague and good friend Professor H. S. Smith (University College London), to whom I wish to express my deep gratitude. I also wish to thank Dr. G. T. Martin (University College London), who gave me much valuable practical aid and advice. Without their help, this project would never have appeared in its present shape. I am grateful also to the authorities of the Griffith Institute, to Dr. Jaromír Málek and Miss Helen Murray for allowing me to consult Gunn's manuscripts, and for permission to publish extracts from them in this work. I also wish to thank Mr. C. J. Eyre of the University of Liverpool for his great help in photographing the whole tomb; he also reproduced Gunn's manuscripts and brought them to my knowledge for the first time. I would like to thank Dr. D. M. Dixon (University College London), and the staff of the Petrie Museum for their help at all times, and to express my special debt to Miss Anthea Page for typing the book. My thanks are extended to the Egypt Exploration Society for the kind permission to publish the plan of the site. I wish also to thank Mr. Peter Harrison of the Central Photographic Service in the University College London who reproduced all my drawings for this book, and I am grateful to Messrs. Aris and Phillips for undertaking the publication of this work while I was in England.

Finally, I wish to record my indebtedness to the British Council for awarding me a scholarship for one year to study in the Department of Egyptology at University College, which enabled me to complete this work, and to Dr. N. A. Daniel, Cultural Attaché at the British Embassy in Cairo for his kindly help and encouragement.

Dr. Shehata Adam, President of the Antiquities Organization of Egypt, generously gave me leave of absence to undertake the present publication.

ABBREVIATIONS

ASAE	*Annales du Service des Antiquités de l'Egypte*.
Gardiner, *Onomastica*	A. H. Gardiner, *Ancient Egyptian Onomastica*, 3 vols., Oxford, 1947.
JAOS	*Journal of the American Oriental Society*.
JEA	*Journal of Egyptian Archaeology*.
MIE	*Memoires des l'Institut d'Egypte*.
P.M.	B. Porter and R. L. B. Moss, *Topographical Bibliography of Ancient Egyptian hieroglyphic texts, reliefs and paintings*, III, 2nd ed. pt. I (Oxford, 1977).
TPC	C. M. Firth and B. Gunn, *Teti pyramid Cemeteries*, 2 vols., Cairo, 1926.
Urk I	K. Sethe, *Urkunden des alten Reiches*, Leipzig, 1903.
Wb	A. Erman and H. Grapow, *Wörterbuch der Aegyptischen Sprache*, 7 vols., Leipzig and Berlin, 1928-63.
ZÄS	*Zeitschrift für Ägyptische Sprache und Altertumskunde*.

LIST OF PLATES AND FIGURES

Numbers in brackets refer to the plan on p.4

List of Text figures

Fig. 1: Location of the tomb.

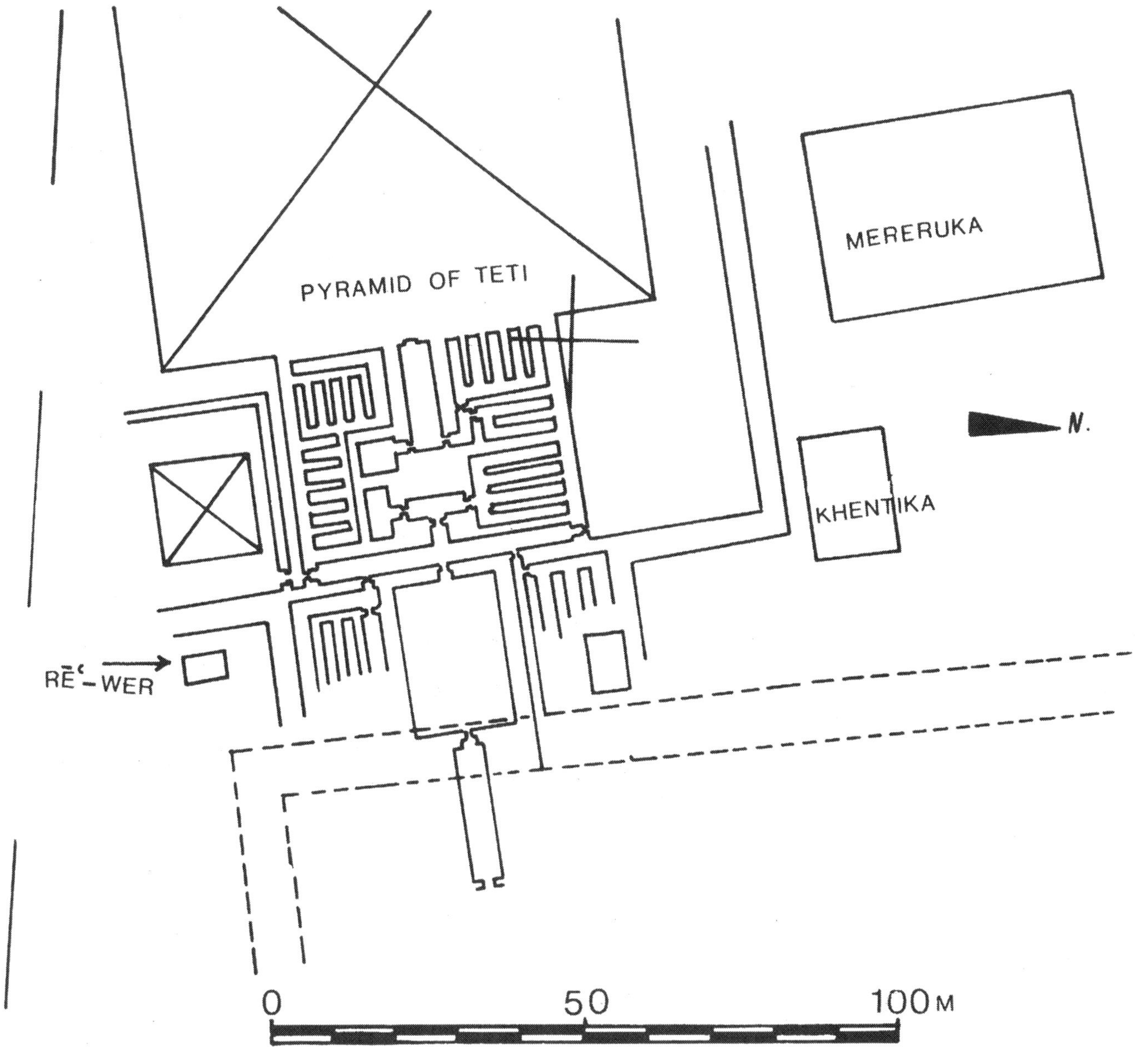

PREFACE TO THE 2024 EDITION

In the 1970s, a much-anticipated new series of publications illustrated objects and themes related to the excavations of the archaeologist William Matthew Flinders Petrie (1853–1942) in Egypt, and aspects of the collection of University College London's Petrie Museum of Egyptian and Sudanese Archaeology. A young couple setting up in business in the early 1970s, Aris and Phillips published these works, written by members of the UCL Egyptology Department, in their *Modern Egyptology* series. Building on Petrie's own observations, the authors of these volumes aimed to complete the great task of publishing the Petrie Museum of Egyptian and Sudanese Archaeology's vast collection, and to present some of the research that Petrie himself was not able to address in his own published works during his lifetime. As the current Curator of the Petrie Museum, it is a great privilege for me to support Oxbow Books in their mission to republish the series, which remains a key source of information for all those interested in object-based approaches to the study of the ancient world.

The Petrie Museum, part of University College London (UCL), is home to one of the largest and most significant collections of Egyptian and Sudanese archaeology in the world. Free to visit, this extraordinary collection tells stories about the lives of ordinary people who lived along the Nile Valley thousands of years ago. Originally set up as a teaching collection, the Petrie Museum comprises over 80,000 objects housed together with an internationally important archaeological archive. It is a collection of world firsts and 'oldests': the oldest woven garment; the oldest worked iron objects; the first known depiction of loom weaving; the oldest known written document about women's health; the earliest veterinary treatise; the oldest will on paper. The Museum has Designated Status from Arts Council England, meaning that it is considered to have outstanding resonance and national cultural significance. The collection has a substantial, visible international reputation for research, supporting hundreds of researchers every year, both remotely and in person.

The Petrie Museum is named after Flinders Petrie, who was appointed in 1892 as the first Professor of Egyptian Archaeology and Philology in the UK at UCL. Over three-quarters of the material in the Museum comes from excavations directed or funded by Petrie, or from purchases he made for university teaching. In 1880 at the age of 26, Petrie travelled to Egypt to survey the Great Pyramid. For the next five decades he was at the forefront of the development of archaeology in Egypt and later in Palestine, and his detailed methodological approach continues to shape the discipline today.

Petrie worked at more sites, with greater speed, than any modern archaeologist: seeing his life as a mission of rescue archaeology, Petrie aimed to retrieve as much information as possible from sites that were shrinking dramatically in size as Egypt modernised during the late 19th and early 20th centuries. He published a large part, but not all, of the finds from his excavations in his illustrated typological volumes, arranged according to object types and themes. Today, much of the Petrie Museum's collection is displayed and stored in a way which reflects these publications: for example, several storage cupboards are dedicated to the material illustrated in the 'Objects of Daily Use' volume, and objects in the drawers are arranged according to the order of the published plates. This offers a unique opportunity for researchers to engage with Petrie's typological and methodical approach to archaeology, as well as with the history of museum collections.

The first catalogue to be published in the *Modern Egyptology* series was *Amarna: City of Akhenaten and Nefertiti* in 1972 by Julia Samson, Petrie Museum Honorary Research Assistant. As official publishers to the UCL Egyptology Department the series went on to produce facsimile reprints of eight of Flinders Petrie's most important site reports and many of his object catalogues, originally published through the British School of Archaeology in Egypt. The substantial annual royalties from these reprints were paid into the 'Petrie Fund' at the time, which provided special grants to students in financial need.

In many ways, the new reprints of this classic series can be seen as the latest layer in a vast 'publication stratigraphy' of the thousands of finds from Flinders Petrie's excavations, which now live in museum collections around the world. On reading these volumes, I hope that readers will also be inspired to learn more about the Petrie Museum collection and its fascinating history.

Dr Anna Garnett
Petrie Museum of Egyptian and Sudanese Archaeology,
University College London
January 2023

PUBLISHER'S PREFACE

Oxbow Books is pleased to present this title in our *Classics in Egyptology* series. This series of facsimile re-issues is comprised of two sub-series. The first consists of 16 typological catalogues produced by W.M. Flinders Petrie based on his massive collection of Egyptian artefacts. Mostly excavated by Petrie during many seasons of campaign in the last years of the 19th and early decades of the 20th century, they now reside in the Petrie Museum at University College London. Published between 1898 and 1937 and long out of print, the catalogues were re-issued in facsimile by publishers Aris and Phillips in the 1970s. These were followed in the next 15 years or so by publication of a number of newly commissioned titles, based on more recent examination of elements of the Petrie Collection by contemporary experts, under the name *Modern Egyptology*. A selection of these additional titles forms the second component of our own series.

The archaeology of Egypt continues to fascinate. Multi-disciplinary investigation and research continues unabated, encompassing methodologies, scientific and data processing techniques, theoretical approaches, and even whole paradigms that were unheard of in the 1970s and undreamt of when Petrie was working in Egypt. Yet all the titles included in this series continue to be invaluable sources of basic data, providing an unparalleled resource that can easily be cross-referenced with the actual materials they describe and discuss. They remain within the Petrie Collection where they may be accessed and re-examined as new research flourishes. As historic documents, the Petrie catalogues stand as exemplars of the craft of typological classification, the backbone of modern archaeology – much of which, though refined by absolute dating and another 100 years of research, still stands the test of time.

A note on presentation

The facsimile titles of Petrie's catalogues re-issued in the 1970s were produced from scans of the original publications. Scanning technology at that time was not of the standard or resolution of today. The scans are no longer available, nor has it been possible to obtain, and in doing so destroy, original copies of the Petrie catalogues. These titles have therefore, of necessity, been rescanned from the 1970s re-issues. Where necessary the pages have been digitally enhanced for clarity of reading and to ensure the good quality of the plates, though inevitably a few are not of the standard we might wish, because of the quality of the previous scan, and occasional blocks of text are not precisely 'straight' or evenly situated on the page. However, some pages in the 1970s re-issues had been inserted in the wrong order and this has been corrected. The originals were produced at a folio size. The pages have been reduced slightly to standard A4 for ease of shelving and because this has the effect of slightly improving the scanned images. In some cases, illustrations were presented to scale and the original scale is given on the plate. There were also no digital files available for titles included in the *Modern Egyptology* series, so these too have been scanned from printed copies.

CHAPTER I

The Tomb of Rēꜥ-wer

Introduction

1. The situation of the tomb

The tomb of Rēꜥ-wer lies at the south-eastern corner of the Mortuary Temple of King Teti, the first king of the Sixth Dynasty (c.2340-2310 B.C.), towards the north end of the Old Kingdom necropolis at Saqqara. It is located east of the subsidiary or ritual pyramid of the Teti complex, outside the enclosure wall of the Mortuary Temple, in the angle where this turns to the east (see Fig. 1).[1]

Its situation therefore corresponds approximately to that of the tomb of Khentika called Ikhekhi, which is at the north-east corner of the Mortuary Temple.[2]

At present, the tomb of Khentika is the nearest mastaba to the tomb of Rēꜥ-wer; it is notable that, despite their favourable position immediately east of the pyramid, both are smaller than the great mastaba-tombs of Mereruka and Kagemni and those of the "the Street of Tombs" to the north of the pyramid.[3] However, to the east and south of the tomb lie great mounds of unexcavated debris, rising higher than the present roof of the tomb by about three metres. These mounds, which separate the tomb of Rēꜥ-wer on the east and south from the modern motor road leading to the office of the Antiquities Service, almost certainly contain the debris of the south-western corner of the great enclosure wall of the temple town of Anubis and the north western corner of the great enclosure wall of the temple town of Bastis. These Late Period temple sites are at present being investigated by the Egypt Exploration Society.[4] (pl. 18, no. B).

From my excavation round the tomb of Rēꜥ-wer it seems probable that further Old Kingdom mastaba-tombs lie under these mounds, and form a further important area of the Teti pyramid cemeteries like that which adjoins the tomb of Khentika.[5]

2. The excavation of the tomb

The original discovery of the tomb

The precise date of the discovery of the tomb of Rēꜥ-wer is not clear. J. E. Quibell excavated the small pyramid on the south of the Mortuary Temple of Teti in 1906-07. His plan and photographs show that he cleared the court east of the small pyramid as far as the inner (west) face of the enclosure wall of the Teti complex, but not the tomb of Rēʿ-wer to the east.[6] Work on the Teti pyramid complex was resumed by C. M. Firth in 1920, when the main excavations were concentrated on the mastabas north of the Teti pyramid Mortuary Temple. In his description of this work, Firth mentions (in his report on the work of 1921-22) the small pyramid and discusses its date. In this passage he states that "there was very little space between its east side and the temenos wall of the Teti pyramid and it is possible that no chapel was ever constructed on the east side. Under the pavement before the east front are two fine sandstone bowls into which the rain-water drained".[7] These bowls had been found by Quibell,[8] so that this passage does not prove that Firth excavated in the region of the small pyramid. However, in the archives of the Griffith Institute there is a notebook of Battiscombe Gunn (Gunn MSS XV.8),[9] Firth's collaborator in his work on the Teti pyramid cemeteries, in which the inscriptions of the tomb of Rēʿ-wer are recorded,[10] and also two statues of the owner and certain blocks from the tomb.[11] It is therefore clear that although Firth makes no reference to the excavation of the tomb of Rēʿ-wer it must have been completely cleared during his excavations, for Gunn to have recorded it. Unfortunately, Gunn's manuscript notebook is not dated, but it must be presumed to have been completed during the excavations at the Teti pyramid before Firth moved on to work on the Step Pyramid in 1924.

Thus the date of excavation was probably between 1920 and 1923. Search in the records of the Antiquities Service at Saqqara has not yielded any trace of Firth's notes on the excavation of the tomb of Rēʿ-wer, though certain other records of Firth's are preserved.

Recent excavation of the Department of Antiquities

In 1975 I started the work of re-excavating the tomb of Rēʿ-wer which had been covered with sand since the previous clearance. In the first season I cleared the sand from the interior and from around the foundation of the tomb (pl. 18, no. C). I found that most of the upper course was missing. I therefore decided to reconstruct the walls of the tomb to their original height to protect it. The restoration of the tomb took two seasons to finish. Of the loose blocks which were found buried in the debris and sand both in and outside the tomb, some came from the walls while others with rounded top belonged to the temenos wall.

In 1977 I cleared the area around the tomb, particularly on the east and south sides. The temenos wall was found in this season, together with some further blocks. Beyond the temenos wall on the east and south high mounds of debris still await excavation (pl. 18, no. A).

3. The Subject of the reliefs

The whole decoration of the tomb of Rēʿ-wer, like that of the other tombs of the period, was apparently designed to sustain the dead man in happiness in the other world. The tomb was the house of the deceased, where he continued his earthly existence. The tomb chapel was however also where the offering cult to his *kꜣ* was to be celebrated in perpetuity. While therefore the scenes of daily life show the daily activities on his estate, they concentrate upon those which provide the offerings, which are shown being carried in profusion to his false-door stelae. Naturally, the most important scenes are those on the west wall which represent two antithetical figures of Rēʿ-wer seated before offering tables, receiving these food offerings, of which the accompanying inscription gives a list.

Fig. 2: Plan of the tomb, showing location of scenes.

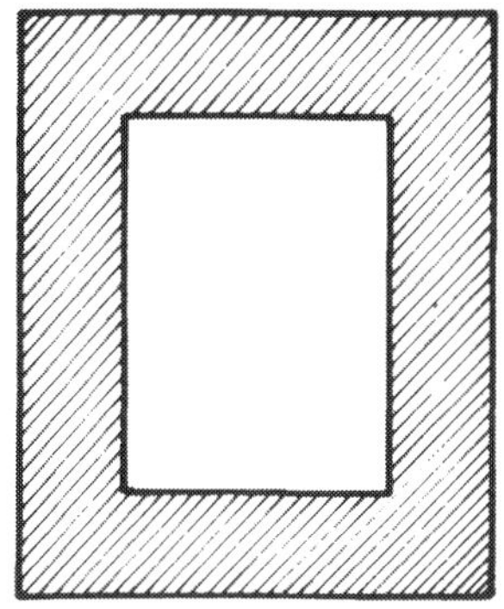

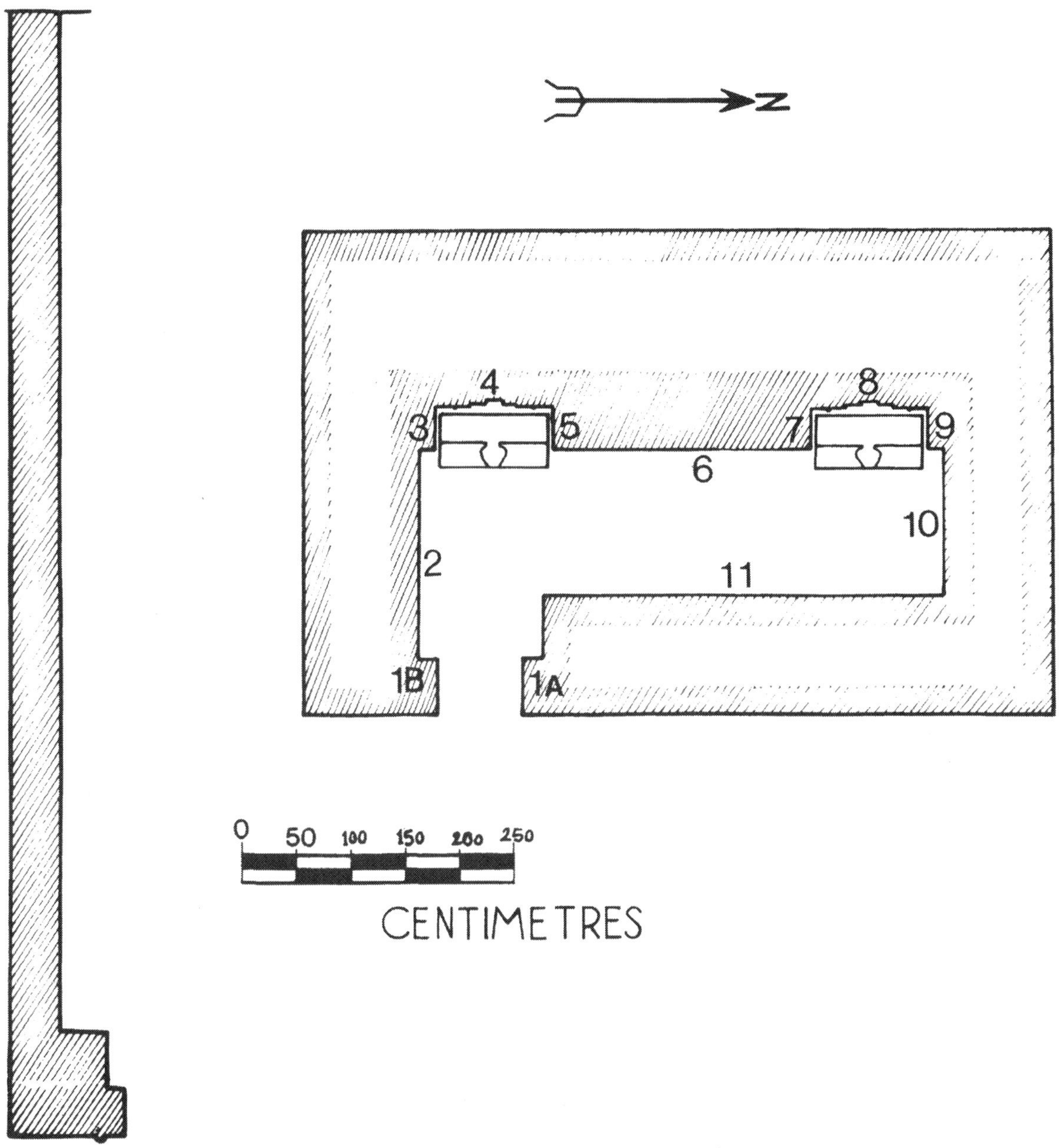

CHAPTER II

The architecture of the tomb and the techniques used

1. General description (Fig. 2).

The tomb of Rēʿ-wer measures 6.83 metres N. to S. and 4.30 metres E. to W. and is 2.20 metres in height on the exterior. It consists of a rectangular chapel which served as the superstructure. The tomb on the interior measures 4.74 metres N. to S. and 1.85 metres E. to W., and is 2.20 metres in height. The tomb is remarkable among those of the group of the Teti pyramid, in having two false-doors in the west wall, both for the use of one person, i.e. the owner of the tomb, the Vizier Rēʿ-wer.[12]

Like other tombs of this group, the tomb of Rēʿ-wer is built within and without of limestone, most of that used inside being of finer texture than the rest. The limestone of fine quality used for lining mastabas was quarried across the Nile just south of Cairo in the quarries of Tura and Ma'sara.[13] The walls appear to have been built course by course, with the ends of the blocks cut first to fit one against another, and the top face levelled off in preparation for the next course after a complete course had been laid.

A mortar, which is presumably gypsum, was used in setting the blocks and in levelling the courses. The same mortar was used as a plaster to fill spaces between the blocks and any breaks or holes in the surface after the walls had been dressed, (pl. 20, nos. 2; 11).

Throughout the tomb the upper part of the walls are lost, except small portions of the north-east corner of the east wall, the two false-doors in the west wall, and north-west corner of the north wall.

When the sculptor began his work, the wall was quite smooth, and the plaster which filled the joints, breaks and holes was carved along with the stone itself. Now most of the plaster has fallen, carrying with it portions of the scenes, and the rest may still be seen *in situ* on the walls, see below.

2. <u>The outside of the mastaba (pl. 18, no. A; B).</u>

The façade of the tomb faces east. On the right hand side of the entrance only one course of the foundation of the tomb remains, from which the last block at the northern corner is missing. However, one block which forms the second course of the north entrance jamb is preserved. The left hand side of the entrance has two courses of white limestone intact, but the upper part of this wall is missing. The northern wall retains one block of local limestone, of which the western end remains intact, but the rest of the wall - as with the other walls - is missing. The western wall has two courses of local limestone: the first course is complete, but the second course is lost at either end, and the middle slabs remain intact. The southern wall has two complete courses of local limestone. The construction technique of the walls of this tomb is as follows: the masons built the external walls of local limestone without mortar, and the internal walls of white limestone using large slabs with mortar. They filled the space between the two walls with small blocks of local stone. The thickness of the walls is as follows:

Eastern wall 1.05 metres.
Northern wall 1.05 metres.
Southern wall 1.05 metres.
Western wall 1.95 metres, a most unusual thickness. A possible explanation for that is that the two false-doors are situated in this wall. There are no remains of any inscriptions on the outer walls.

3. <u>The courtyard and the pavement (pl. 18, no. A).</u>

In front of the façade of the tomb, which as usual faces east, is the courtyard. Only the measurements of the south-east corner are available, because the rest of it is covered with sand and debris. The original measurement of the courtyard can however be calculated, and was 3.48 metres E. to W. and 11.33 metres N. to S. (see below).

The pavement is a patchwork of approximately rectangular limestone slabs. Most of these slabs around the front edge of the walls pass under the walls, and were therefore laid first, but in the east and west walls it appears that the slabs were laid after the wall had been erected. This perhaps suggests that the east wall was built first to give the north-south alignment of the tomb. Then the pavement of the chapel and courtyard was laid, and finally, the remaining walls of the tomb were built on this base. Some of these pavement slabs have been taken away, particularly at the entrance and in the courtyard of the tomb.

4. <u>The temenos wall and the courtyard (pl. 18, no. A; Fig. 2).</u>

After clearing the sand and debris from the south side of the tomb, the foundations of the temenos wall were uncovered. Only the southern arm and the south-east corner of the wall are preserved (see Fig. 2). The eastern wall ends with the stepped-back reveal of an entrance. The southern arm measures 10.0 metres in length, 0.45 metres in width and 0.88 metres in height. The eastern wall is 1.05 metres long, 0.57 metres wide and 0.88 metres high. The internal reveal measures 15 cm. E. to W. by 16 cm. N. to S., and is set back 42 cm. from the east face of the wall. The south internal jamb of this gate is only 43 cm. from the north face of the south temenos wall. On the outer (east) face of the east wall is a vertical torus moulding which evidently surrounded the door; this is set 17 cm. from the jamb of the gate.

While this is all that is preserved of the temenos wall, it is evident from this gate-jamb that the wall must have continued on the north side of the gate. As the southern arm of the temenos wall is 2.25 metres from the south external wall of the tomb, it is probable that the northern arm was at a similar distance from the north external wall of the tomb. If so, the internal measurements of the courtyard would have been 11.33 metres from N. to S. Many blocks from this temenos wall have been found in the debris, and some may have been taken to be reused. Among them are blocks with rounded tops which must have formed the crest of the wall, as is not uncommon in surround walls.[14] A lintel found lying on the pavement in the gate through the temenos wall should belong to this gate: it is certainly too large to fit the main entrance to the tomb. Thus it gives the approximate width of the gate: (1.75 m. long, 0.42 m. wide and 0.50 m. high).

Firth has suggested that all the great Sixth Dynasty tombs in the Teti pyramid complex were originally protected by temenos walls.[15] It is doubtful, however, whether in all cases such a temenos wall completely surrounded the tomb: the evidence from Mereruka suggests that the wall was present only on the south side of the tomb, forming a court in front of the entrance.[16]

At the mastaba of Khentika, the temenos wall runs on the eastern side parallel with the facade, but does not surround the tomb.[17] But in the mastaba of Rēʿ-wer, the temenos wall certainly seems likely to have surrounded the tomb on three sides; it is possible that the east wall of the pyramid temple formed the west wall of Rēʿ-wer's temenos wall. It is to be noted that the gate through the temenos is not in alignment with the main entrance of the tomb.

5. The roof

The original roof and the upper courses of the walls in the tomb are missing. One may assume that the roof was constructed of limestone. It probably consisted of simple slabs because it is a very narrow tomb (see pl. 18, no. C), and these slabs would rest directly on the tops of the walls.

The tomb was probably lit by two(?) openings left in the slabs of the roof, each opening being above a false-door, so that some sunlight would penetrate into the tomb to illuminate its most important features.

6. The shaft (Fig. 2; pl. 18, no. B).

To the back of the west wall of the tomb of Rēʿ-wer, and at a distance of 3.73 metres from it, is a shaft which is presumably that belonging to the tomb. It measures 1.40 N. to S. and 2.20 E. to W., and is 6.90 metres deep. It was cut out of the local rock, all four sides being left in the rough. The mouth of the shaft was recessed to take the slab which closed it (see pl. 18, no. B). This shaft was cleared during Firth's work in this area, but when I recleared it because it was filled with sand and debris, I found it completely empty. Gunn does not mention anything about the shaft in his notes.

At the bottom of the shaft there are chambers on three sides. The principal chamber, which lies in the western side of the shaft, is the only one which is carefully cut in the natural rock. It is rectangular, measuring 3.60 metres long, 2.55 metres wide, and 1.05 metres high. Along the western wall of this chamber, at a height of 30 cm. from the floor, is a rock-cut shelf. Although nothing was found in this chamber, and there were no traces of a sarcophagus nor any blocks nor objects, it seems possible that it had been used as a burial chamber.

In the northern wall of the shaft is the entrance to the second chamber, which is roughly cut in the rock and unfinished. The state of the rock in which this chamber was cut is very fragile, so that in many places masses of it had fallen. It measures 2.85 metres in length, 2.35 metres in width and 1.0 metres in height. In the western side is an entrance leading to another small chamber, unfinished and roughly cut, which measures 1.90 by 1.80 by 1.0 metres. During clearance nothing was found.

In the eastern wall of the main shaft lies the last small chamber, which measures 2.20 metres long, 1.40 metres wide and 0.90 metres high. This chamber was also empty.

7. The interior

The tomb is entered through a door in its east wall. This door is off-centre, its south jamb being 1.24 metres from the south-east external corner of the tomb. The motive for placing the door in this corner is probably a desire that it should face the principal false-door of the tomb, which is sited at the south end of the west wall, 1.85 metres from the south-west internal corner. As the main axis of the tomb is from north-south, and the interior consists of a single rectangular chamber, it is natural that the two false-doors should have been placed at either end of the west wall. The northern false-door is 1.27 metres from the interior north-west corner of the chamber.

The plan of the interior of the chamber (Fig. 2) shows its dimensions, the location of the scenes, and the position of the false-doors. The structure of each internal wall is shown in a schematic elevation (Figs. 3-9). The details of the false-doors may be understood from the numbered plans and elevations (Figs. 2; 5; 7), which also serve as a key to the numbering of the inscriptions upon them. When found, the walls of the tomb were preserved to an average height of 2.20 metres. The height of the original roof from the floor of the interior can be estimated with reasonable accuracy from the proportions of the figures of Rēʿ-wer on the west wall, and from the positions of the tops of the main door-jambs and of the false-door.

8. The colours (pl. 20B; 21.8).

The principal colours in the tomb of Rēʿ-wer are red and green pigments. The red colour was used on the figures (all male) in the scenes, but it is only on the south wall that it is still visible to any extent. It is also used on the north false-door in imitation of granite. The green pigment was used to fill the hieroglyphic texts on the north false-door. As a whole the colour in this tomb is not well preserved, and not all the walls of the mastaba appear to have been painted.

9. The restoration of the tomb (pl. 18A and B).

The Department of Antiquities undertook extensive work in restoring the tomb of Rēʿ-wer in 1976-7, using new materials in the restoration. In these times, it is too difficult to use blocks of white limestone of the same size as the originals in the restoration, so small local limestone blocks were used in restoring the exterior walls of the tomb, using mud mortar, which can easily be moved should the original blocks be found later. For the lintel of the entrance of the tomb (the original lintel is missing) concrete slabs were used, plastered with gypsum to imitate the limestone. To reconstruct the upper course of the walls in the interior of the tomb, another kind of well-dressed white limestone was used. The restored upper course is of the same height as the original (about 50 cm.), so that all the walls of the tomb are now restored to their original height.

The original roof of the tomb is missing, so a modern roof was placed in position consisting of six concrete slabs resting directly on the tops of the reconstructed walls, coloured on the interior with gypsum to imitate limestone. Two rectangular openings were left in the reconstructed slabs of the roof, so that some sunlight may penetrate into the tomb (pl. 18, no. A).

Two blocks were found buried in the sand on the south side of the tomb: these appear to have formed the upper course of both entrance door jambs (pl. 19, nos. 1A; 1B). These blocks fit these jambs exactly, and complete the scene on the panel representing the owner of the tomb as a standing figure moving out of the tomb, with above him seven vertical lines with his titles in raised relief. The block from the northern jamb is divided into two pieces, measuring 30 x 43 cms. and 21 x 43 cms. The block from the southern jamb measures 51 x 49 cms. In the interior of the tomb certain blocks which had come out of alignment were adjusted to position them correctly in relation to the remainder of the wall scene. The offering table in front of the northern false-door was restored to its correct position.

CHAPTER III

The reliefs and inscriptions

1. Titles and epithets of Rēꜥ-wer

1.	*i͗ry-pꜥt*	Hereditary prince
2.	*ḥꜣty-ꜥ*	The Count
3.	*tꜣyty sꜣb ṯꜣty*	The Shrouded one, judge and vizier
4.	*ẖry-ḥbt ḥry-tp*	Chief Lector priest
5.	*i͗mꜣ-ꜥ*	Agreeable of hand
6.	*smsw snwt*	Elder of the Snwt-house
7.	*sm*	Sm-priest
8.	*ḫrp šmdt nbt*	Controller of every kilt
9.	*ꜥḏ-mr Dp*	Nome administrator of Buto
10.	*sḏꜣwty-bi͗ty*	Treasurer of the King of Lower Egypt
11.	*i͗my-r šmꜥ*	Overseer of Upper Egypt
12.	*smr wꜥty*	Sole Companion
13.	*i͗mꜣḫw ḫr nṯr ꜥꜣ*	Honoured by the great god
14.	*i͗mꜣḫw ḫr I͗npw tpy ḏw.f*	Honoured by Anubis who presides over his mountain
15.	*i͗mꜣḫw ḫr nṯrw šmꜥ*	Honoured by the gods of Upper Egypt
16.	*mry-nṯr*	Beloved of the god

2. <u>The entrance: north door-jamb (pl. 1; pl. 19A; Fig. 3).</u>

Fig. 3: Masonry at entrance. Scale 1:20

1A 1B

On the right hand side of the entrance to the tomb is a scene on the right door-jamb representing the owner moving out of the tomb (1A on plan, p. 4 above). The carving of the figure of the deceased and the hieroglyphic inscriptions above him are in raised relief. Both the figure and the inscriptions are in a very good state of preservation, and are well carved.[18] If the superior carving and workmanship of these two entrance door-jambs is compared with the carving of scenes in other parts of the tomb, it would appear that the hand of a different artist finished these. So it seems that more than one artist may have worked in the tomb.

The principal figure in this panel which measures 97 x 37 cms. is the deceased. He is represented as a standing figure holding a long straight staff in his left hand. He is wearing a shoulder-length wig, and a flaring kilt reaching to the knee. It is formed of a single piece of cloth wrapped round the body, draped high at the back and low at the front, and tied at the waist (the tie is damaged, but visible). A sceptre, with its head in the form of an open papyrus-flower below the baton, is in his right hand. Round his neck he wears a broad collar (*wsḫ*) formed of several rows of beads, and the scarf of office is bound across his left shoulder and tucked under his right shoulder. The face has been deliberately hacked out with a chisel. He walks barefoot. The representation of the deceased on the entrance door-jambs in this attitude is very common in Old Kingdom mastabas and rock-tombs.

Before him, his name was inscribed in incised relief but has been scratched out. There remain the initial signs of his name Rēʿ-(wer). Over the head of the deceased are seven well carved vertical lines of titles. These lines, numbered 1 to 7, read from right as follows:

1. *ỉry-pʿt*[19] *ḥ3ty-ʿ, t3yty s3b ṯ3ty*[20]

The hereditary prince, the Count, the shrouded one, judge, and vizier.

2. *ẖry-ḥb(t) ḥry-tp, ỉm3-ʿ,*[21] *smsw snw(t).*[22]

The Chief lector priest, agreeable of hand, the elder of the *Snwt*-house.

3. *sm,*[23] *ḫrp šndt nb(t), ʿḏ-mr*[24] *Dp*

The *Sm*-priest, the Controller of every kilt, the nome administrator of Buto.

4. *sḏ3wty-bỉty, ỉmy-r šmʿ*

The treasurer of the king of Lower Egypt, the overseer of Upper Egypt.

5. *(ỉm3)ḫw ḫr nṯr ʿ3*

The one honoured before the great god.

6. *(ỉm3)ḫw ḫr 'Inpw tpy-ḏw.f*

The one honoured before Anubis who presides over his mountain.

7. Text missing.

3. The entrance: south door-jamb (pl. 2; pl. 19B; Fig. 3).

On the left hand side of the entrance of the tomb is the panel of the south door jamb which measures 97 x 37 cms. (pl. 2, pl. 19, no. B). The owner of the tomb is represented on the panel moving out of the tomb (lB on plan, p. 4 above). The jamb is almost as well preserved as the north jamb, though the feet are missing. The figure of Reʿ-wer and the hieroglyphs above him are in raised relief, and are well-carved.[25]

The deceased is represented as a standing figure holding a long straight staff in his left hand.[26] He is wearing a shoulder-lenth wig, and a flaring kilt reaching to the knees, holding the *sḫm* sceptre, with a papyrus-flower below the baton, in his left hand. He wears the scarf of office across his right shoulder and tucked under his left shoulder. The face of Rēʿ-wer has been scratched out, and so have some parts of his body.[27] Before the standing figure of the deceased his name and title are also obliterated. The text, in incised relief, reads:

Over the head of the deceased are seven vertical lines of titles, well-carved. These lines, numbered 1 to 7, read from left to right as follows:

1. *(ỉry-pꜥt), ḥꜣty-ꜥ, tꜣyty sꜣb ṯꜣty*

   The hereditary prince, the Count, the shrouded one, judge, and vizier.

2. *(ẖry-ḥb(t)) ḥry-tp, ỉmꜣ-ꜥ, smsw snw(t)*

   The Chief lector priest, Agreeable of hand, the elder of the *Snwt*-house.

3. *sm, ḫrp šndt nbt, ꜥḏ-mr Dp*

   The *Sm*-priest, the controller of every kilt, the nome-administrator of Buto.

4. *sḏꜣwty-bỉty, ỉmy-r šmꜥ*

   The treasurer of the king of Lower Egypt, the overseer of Upper Egypt.

5. *ỉmꜣḫw ḫr Ỉnpw tpy-ḏw.f*

   The one honoured before Anubis who presides over his mountain.

6. *ỉmꜣḫw ḫr nṯr ꜥꜣ*

   The one honoured before the great god.

7. *....mry ...?*

   (The text is missing).

4. <u>The South wall (pl. 3; pl. 20B).</u>

Fig. 4: Masonry of South Wall (top course reconstructed). Scale 1:20

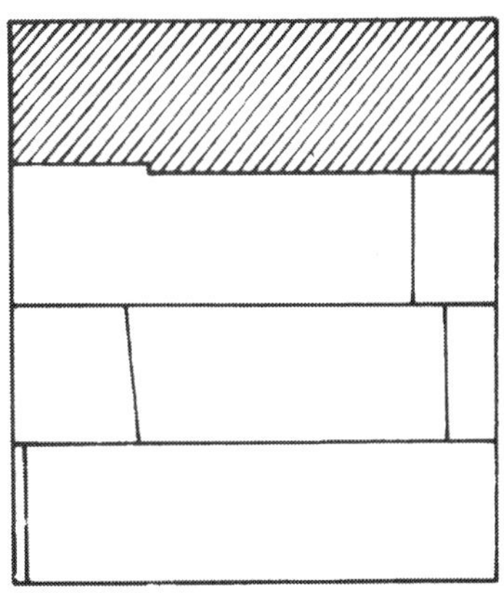

The south wall measures 1.78 metres in length and 1.47 metres in height, and consists of three courses of masonry. Originally there were four courses, but the upper course is now missing (Fig. 4). Four registers occupy this wall; the topmost is missing. The principal figure is, as is customary, at the west end of the wall nearest the stela or the false-door.

There are holes all over this wall, particularly on the faces of the figures. Red pigment can still be seen on the figures of the offering-bearers (pl. 20B). The representations on the wall begin at a distance of 70 cms. west of the south-east corner, leaving an undecorated space corresponding to the size of the doorway in the east wall. There is a door socket in the threshold of this entrance by the south door-jamb, while the hole for the attachment of the door-bolt is in the north jamb. Thus when opened, the door would have swung back against the eastern portion of the inner south wall. This is no doubt the reason why its decoration was considered superfluous. The deceased was represented in raised relief but the offering-bearers are in outline. The south wall is less well-preserved than the north wall, the inscription in front of the deceased also being broken in some parts. The representation of the deceased is slightly different in pose from that of the north wall. In the south wall the owner of the tomb was represented as a standing figure holding a long straight staff, probably in his left hand, and a sceptre with its head in the form of an open papyrus-flower below the baton in his left hand.[28] He wears a flaring kilt reaching to the knees; it is formed of a single piece of cloth wrapped round the body, draped high at the back and low at the front, and tied at the waist. He is barefoot. There is the lower part of a broad collar around his neck and a bracelet on his surviving left wrist (pl. 3).

The inscriptions in front of the standing figure of the deceased are in raised relief, and are broken in some places. The vertical line reads as follows:

...*(ỉ)nnt n.f m ḥwt.f m nỉwt.f nt*[29] *tꜣ-mḥw šmꜥw, prt-ḫrw t ḥnḳt n.f ỉm*

..... which are brought to him from his estates, and from his towns of Lower and Upper Egypt, that invocation offerings of bread and beer may come forth to him there.

Before the standing figure of the deceased there are four registers occupying this wall, the movement of the figures being to the west in the direction of the south false-door. All males who follow are dressed alike in short kilts with side-wrap and short wigs. In these registers none of the figures is named.

The remains of the upper register (the first) can still be seen, showing the bases of offering tables, vases, jars, boxes and bread.

In the second register are five men (the position of the hands in this scene differs from that on the north wall), walking in procession and carrying offerings to the deceased. The first carries a tray laden with bread and cakes on his left shoulder and lotus blossoms and bundles hang from the left arm. In his right hand he holds a live bird by its wings. The next carries on his left shoulder a covered dish and a basket, with papyrus stems on it, hanging from the left arm. He also holds a live bird by its wings in his right hand. The third carries on his left shoulder a tray laden with bread and loaves, papyrus stems hang from the left arm, and he holds a live bird by its wings in his right hand. Then comes a man carrying a bunch of papyrus stalks, entwined with a lotus in his left arm. The bud which he carries has the flexible stalk looped around his hand, and across his right arm he carries a semi-circular object(?), and papyrus stems hang from his right arm. The last figure in this procession is the fifth man, who carries a tray with bread and vases on his left shoulder. A large basket hangs from his left elbow, and he holds a jar by a handle with his right arm.

In the third register are four men who carry birds, and hold them by their wings with the left hand and wring their necks to sacrifice them with their out-stretched right arms. The men grasp the heads of the birds with an action full of energy, and this is one of the few instances in which an artist of the Old Kingdom has succeeded in showing the object clasped within the grasping hand. In the lowest register, (the fourth), four men carry haunches of meat.[30]

In the representation of the offering bearers on the south wall, we can see that some lines are missing, which the sculptor forgot to carve. The horizontal lines of the kilt of the last figure in the second register have not been carved. In other cases the draftsman (or the sculptor) corrected the guiding lines of the figures (see, for instance, figures nos. 3-4 in the second register). Sometimes the artist failed to join the lines of the figures or the offerings which they carry (pl. 20, no. B). This probably shows, as mentioned above, that more than one artist worked on this tomb.

5. The West wall (pls. 4-9).

A. General

The west wall measures 4.74 metres in length, and consists of three horizontal courses occupying a height of 1.54 metres. It is occupied by twin false-door stelae at either end and a scene between them. These two false-doors are preserved to their original height, which is 2.03 metres above the pavement. The wall between is 1.55 metres high. Both false-doors are formed from a single block of white limestone, and both belong to the owner of the tomb, Rēʿ-wer. They are well-preserved. In front of each false-door, projecting into the tomb, is an offering-table carved from a single block of limestone measuring 1.04 x 0.50 x 0.47 metres, with badly worn surfaces showing the *ḥtp* sign on the top. (Fig. 2, nos. 3-9).

The two false-doors (Fig. 5) consist of upper and lower lintels (A, C); a panel (B), four jambs (E-F-G-H), a drum (D), a cavetto cornice (I), and torus moulding (J).

A	Upper lintel :	1.45 x 0.69 m.
B	Panel :	34 x 16 cms.
C	Lower lintel :	42.5 x 11.5 cms.
D	Drum :	13.5 x 7 cms.
E	Outer left jamb :	0.13 x 1.10 m.
F	Inner left jamb :	14 x 82 cms.
G	Outer right jamb :	0.13 x 1.10 m.
H	Inner right jamb :	14 x 82 cms.
I	Cornice :	uncertain
J	Torus :	4 x 3 cms.

Fig. 5: South false-door, plan and sections. Scale 1:20

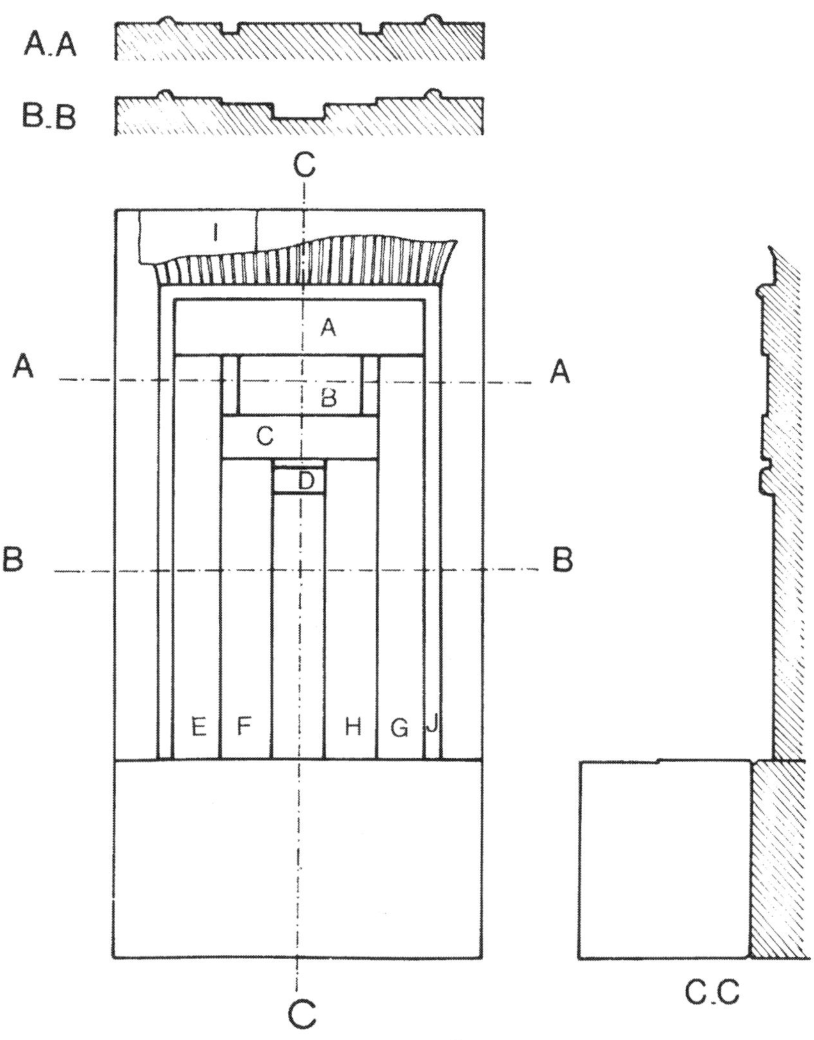

The doors are inscribed with incised hieroglyphs. The panel (B) has scenes in incised relief. The two false-doors are framed at the top and both sides by a torus-moulding which is broken in places, and which is surmounted by a cornice sculpted with incised lines (pl. 21, nos. 4, 8). On the drums of the false-doors (D), the principal titles of Reʿ-wer are given, together with his name. The figures at the bottom of the four jambs, which represent the owner of the tomb, standing and facing inwards towards the niche of the door, are all in incised relief. The figures are alike on both doors, the only difference being that those on the north false-door represent the deceased as a standing figure holding a long straight staff in his right hand, and a papyrus sceptre in the left hand, while in the other (south) false-door he is represented as a standing figure holding a long straight staff in his left hand, and a piece of cloth in his right hand.

On both jambs of the false-doors are incised scenes showing horizontal rows of vessels, inscribed with the names of the seven sacred oils.

B. <u>South false-door (pl. 5; pl. 21, no. 4; Fig. 5)</u>.

The false-door measures 1.47 x 1.01 x 0.53 metres. It is formed from a single block of fine white limestone, and lies at the far south end of the west wall, facing the entrance of the tomb (4 on plan p. 4 above). It consists of upper and lower lintels, a panel, a drum, and four jambs, and is in a very good state of preservation. The inscriptions are in incised relief and well carved, and the workmanship is very good. Some parts are broken, the name of the owner being scratched out as usual in this tomb. The false-door is framed at the top and sides by a torus-moulding which is broken on both sides, and is surmounted by a cornice sculpted with vertical incised double lines, broken at its top edge. At the bottom of each of the four jambs is a small figure of the deceased, standing and facing inwards towards the niche of the door. These figures represent Reʿ-wer standing and holding the long straight staff in his right hand and a piece of cloth in his left hand. He wears a long wig, necklaces and a flaring kilt. The two figures on the left jambs are bigger than those on the right. Below each figure are three horizontal incised lines. The name of the deceased Reʿ-wer has been erased, although the remains of the name can still be seen (pl. 5; pl. 21, no. 4). No traces of colour are visible. The table of offerings (Fig. 5; pl. 21, no. 4) was at the foot of the stela, made from one limestone block with a badly damaged surface, and measuring 1.05 x 50 x 47 metres. It shows a *ḥtp* sign in raised relief.

D : *ḥ3ty-ʿ Rʿ-wr*

The Count Reʿ-wer

B : The deceased is represented as a seated figure. Before him his name has been scratched out, leaving legible traces. The offering table before him is laden with upright slices of bread, and other offerings such as loaves, vegetables, bread, cakes, jars and lettuces. It measures 34 cms. in width and 16 cms. in height.

A : *ḥtp dỉ nsw, ḥtp dỉ ỉnpw tpy ḏw.f prt ḫrw t ḥnḳt n.f hrw nb, ỉry pꜥt Rꜥ-wr.*

A boon which the king gives, and a boon which Anubis, who presides over his mountain, gives that there may be made invocation offerings consisting of bread and beer every day for him, the hereditary prince Rēꜥ-wer.

C : *ỉmy-r šmꜥ, smr wꜥty, mry nṯr, Rꜥ-wr*

Overseer of Upper Egypt, the sole companion, the beloved of the god Rēꜥ-wer.

E : *ḥtp dỉ Wsỉr nb Ḏdw ḫp.f r ỉmntt nfrt, mry nṯr Rꜥ-wr*

A book which Osiris, lord of Busiris,gives, that he may go to the beautiful west, the beloved of the god Rēꜥ-wer.

G : *ḥtp dỉ ỉnpw ỉmy wt ḫp.f m ḥtp r s(mt) ỉmntt, sḏꜣwty-bỉty Rꜥ-wr*[31]

A boon which Anubis who is in the bandage gives, that he may go in peace to the western desert, the treasurer of the king of Lower Egypt Rēꜥ-wer.

F : *ỉmꜣḫw ḫr nṯr ꜥꜣ, mry nṯr Rꜥ-wr.*

Honoured by the great god, beloved of the god Rēꜥ-wer.

H : *ỉmꜣḫw ḫr nṯrw šmꜥ mry nṯr Rꜥ-wr*

Honoured by the gods of Upper Egypt, beloved of the god Rēꜥ-wer.

C. <u>Jambs of the south false-doors (pl. 4, nos. 3, 5)</u>.

On both jambs of the southern false-door are seven incised horizontal lines of hieroglyphs giving the names of the seven sacred oils, contained in the jars represented:

<u>The south jamb (pl. 4, no. 3) (from the top).</u>

1. The name of the first sacred oil is badly damaged.

2. *ḥknw :* A sacred oil. This is one of the oils mentioned in the Book of the Dead. Jéquier considers it as a natural oil,[32] perhaps of vegetable origin, having similar properties to incense, and like that product, found in the South. But a late inscription of Edfu gives detailed instructions for its manufacture, a complicated process which occupied eleven days. Maspero calls it "par-

fum d'acclamation".

3. *sfṯ* : A sacred oil. Determined with the *ḫnm*-vases. Maspero thinks it was of a semi-liquid consistency, not so thin as a true oil, nor so thick as ointment.[33]

4. *nḫnm* : A sacred oil. Maspero suggests that this oil was entirely liquid, because it is represented as being contained in a flask with a narrow neck and a short spout.[34] According to Jéquier, this was a toilet water.

5. *twȝtw* : A sacred oil. Maspero calls this the "parfum de Salut".[35] According to an inscription at Edfu, it was made from the oil *mn*(?)  , goose-grease and a vegetable substance. Jéquier says that the name "perfume of salutation" is meaningless to us.

6. *ḥȝtt ꜥš*[36] : Finest oil of *ꜥš*-wood.

7. *ḥȝtt ṯḥnw*[37] : Finest Libyan oil. This, the last of the seven sacred oils, is usually translated as Libyan oil, and as Libya was also called "the olive-land" one assumes that this was in reality olive-oil.[38] But according to an inscription at Edfu, it was composed of *mn*-oil and acacia flowers (see Jéquier, Frises d'Objets, p. 149).

The north jamb (pl. 4, no. 5).

On the right jamb there survive five sacred oils, since the first two are missing. Reading from the top:

3. Remains of *sfṯ* : A sacred oil.

4. *nḫnm* : A sacred oil.

5. *twȝtw* : A sacred oil.

6. *ḥȝtt ꜥš* : Finest oil of *ꜥš*-wood.

7. *ḥȝtt ṯḥnw* : Finest Libyan oil.

D. The central scene (pls. 6; 7; 22; Fig. 6).

Fig. 6: Masonry of West wall between false-doors, showing location of scenes (top course reconstructed).

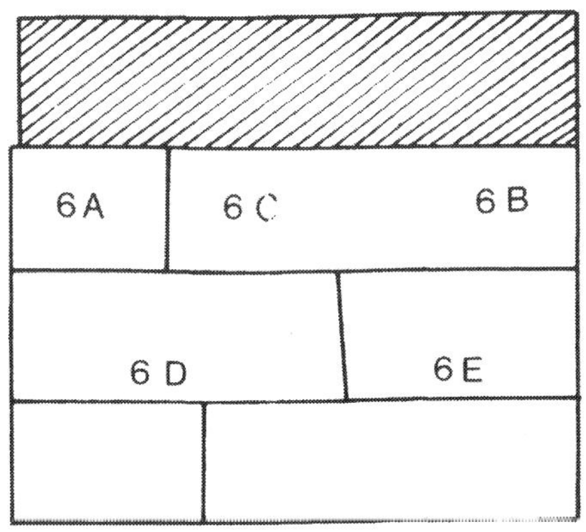

Scale 1:20

The wall which lies between the two false-doors measures 2.32 by 1.54 metres consisting of three courses of yellow limestone, of which the upper is missing. It is the best-preserved wall in the tomb, and the scene which occupies this wall is in raised relief. The workmanship is fine. The scene which decorated this wall consists of two registers, and is a common scene in Old Kingdom mastabas found on the walls of the stela chapel, representing the deceased seated and receiving offerings.

Because the deceased is represented on both sides, this scene is divided in the present publication into several numbered sections. The main divisions of the wall are as follows (Fig. 6): The first register contains nos. 6A, 6B and 6C; the second register contains nos. 6D and 6E.

No. 6A : Represents the owner of the tomb seated on a chair with lion's paw legs and a cushion at his back. His dress is a short close-fitting kilt tied at the waist; his right hand is stretched towards the table, which is laden with conventionalized slices of bread, and his left hand is raised to his face; he wears bracelets on his arms. Below the offering-table and before the deceased an inscription asserts that a thousand of each of the principal offerings are at his disposal. It reads:

ḫꜣ t ḫꜣ snw ḫꜣ ḥnḳt

ḫꜣ kꜣ   ḫꜣ ꜣpd

ḫꜣ šs   ḫꜣ mnḫt

"A thousand loaves of bread, a thousand cakes, a thousand jars of beer, a thousand oxen, a thousand fowl, a thousand alabaster vessels, a thousand pieces of cloth".

Beneath the other side of the offering-table are placed two wooden tables with ewers and basins to facilitate the washing of the hands. These two vessels are in the shape of certain copper vessels found in the tombs of the First Dynasty, and the Old Kingdom. They were of a standard shape for use in the funerary offering and libation ritual. Below the chair, the name *Mnṯw-ḥtp* is carved in very poor hieroglyphs; it is a graffito, probably left by a visitor in the Middle Kingdom. It reads:

No. 6B : The deceased is represented as a seated figure on a chair with lion's paw legs and cushion at his back. He wears a short close-fitting kilt, and a bracelet on each(?) arm. His right hand is stretched out to the table of offerings, his left hand rests on his leg and holds an object resembling a folded piece of cloth(?). Before him is the word 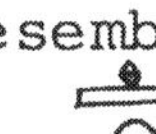 *ḥtp*: "offering". Between the offering table and the deceased an inscription asserts that a thousand of each of the principal offerings are at his disposal. It reads:

ḫꜣ t   ḫꜣ snw   ḫꜣ ḥnḳt

ḫꜣ kꜣ   ḫꜣ ꜣpd

ḫꜣ šs   ḫꜣ mnḫt

"A thousand loaves of bread, a thousand cakes, a thousand jars of beer, a thousand oxen, a thousand fowl, a thousand alabaster vessels, a thousand pieces of cloth".

Under the offering table and before the deceased are two copper ewers and basins of the same type as in scene 6A on low wooden tables. On the other side of the offering table and under it are three big jars, probably of water, in a stand.

No. 6C : The central offering. Between the two figures of the deceased which are carved at each end of this wall is a heap of offerings piled up in confusion, supported upon two low tables on either side of a higher stand. It consists of birds, haunches of oxen, bread, cakes, joints of meat, loaves, lettuces, trays laden with offerings and large loaves. Under the table are haunches of meat, and sealed jars resting in pot-stands.

No. 6D : Seven offering bearers occupy the second (lower) register, in a procession. They move to the south in the direction of the southern false-door, and are below the seated figure of the deceased (6A). All the men wear a short kilt, and figures numbers 3-7 have peculiar wigs. This register is headed at its left end by a vertical inscription which is broken in some parts. It reads:

(sḫp)t stpwt ꜣpdw

"bringing up the choicest haunches and fowl".

The first four men bring the *ḫpš*, the haunch which is the choicest joint of the sacrificial victim and which was offered in the Opening of the Mouth ritual. None of them are named, the other three who follow them carry birds for sacrifice. They grasp the heads of the birds in a manner similar to a scene on the south wall, q.v. Above the last two figures are their names, roughly scratched on the stone as though by an unskilled hand. The sixth is named 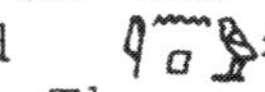 *'Inpw-ḥtp*, and this may be a late inscription. The seventh is named *ỉpy n ...(?) nb.*[39]  Perhaps he is the personage who leads the next group of offering-bearers since he bears the same name.

No. 6E : Below the deceased in 6B, and in the second register, another seven men move in the direction of the northern false-door and bear offerings to the owner of the tomb. All are dressed alike in short kilts, but wear different wigs, the latter being unfinished. A vertical line of text in raised relief heads them, at the right end, and reading:

sḫpt stpwt ꜣpdw

"bringing up the choicest of haunches and fowl".

Only the first man is named, his name written under the haunch of meat, in front of him, again in very poor hieroglyphs:

 , perhaps inserted later.

The marks of the chisels which the artists used in carving the reliefs may still be seen as lines below the second register. The artist in some parts of this wall failed to join the vertical encasing lines. Pitted holes covered most of the scene, particularly over the faces, hands, and feet of the figures of the owner of the tomb (pl. 22).

E. North false-door (pl. 9; pl. 21, no. 8; Fig. 7)

The false-door measures 1.47 x 1.07 x 60 metres, and is formed of a single block of yellow limestone set in the west wall. The workmanship is different from that of the southern stela. The inscriptions are in incised relief, and the name of the deceased has been scratched out systematically. The false-door is framed at the top and two sides by a torus-moulding, which is broken on the left side, and by a cornice broken in places and sculpted with vertical incised lines. At the bottom of the four jambs is a small figure of the deceased standing and facing inwards towards the niche of the door. Rēꜥ-wer stands holding a long straight staff in his right hand and a papyrus sceptre in his other hand.[40] There is a hole in the bottom of the left jamb. All the upper surface of the northern false-door is painted red to imitate granite, the hieroglyphs and the figures of the deceased at the top being incised and coloured with green pigment.[41] (pl. 21, no. 8). The figures of the deceased at the base of the stela are also incised and painted red. The cornice at the top (S) and the torus which surrounds the door at the top and two sides (T) is painted red. At the bottom of these four jambs the craftsman changed his mind for some reason when he sculpted the titles of the deceased and coloured these using a dark red pigment. Perhaps this was in order to hide the original carving (see below).

Fig. 7: North false-door, plan and sections. Scale 1:20

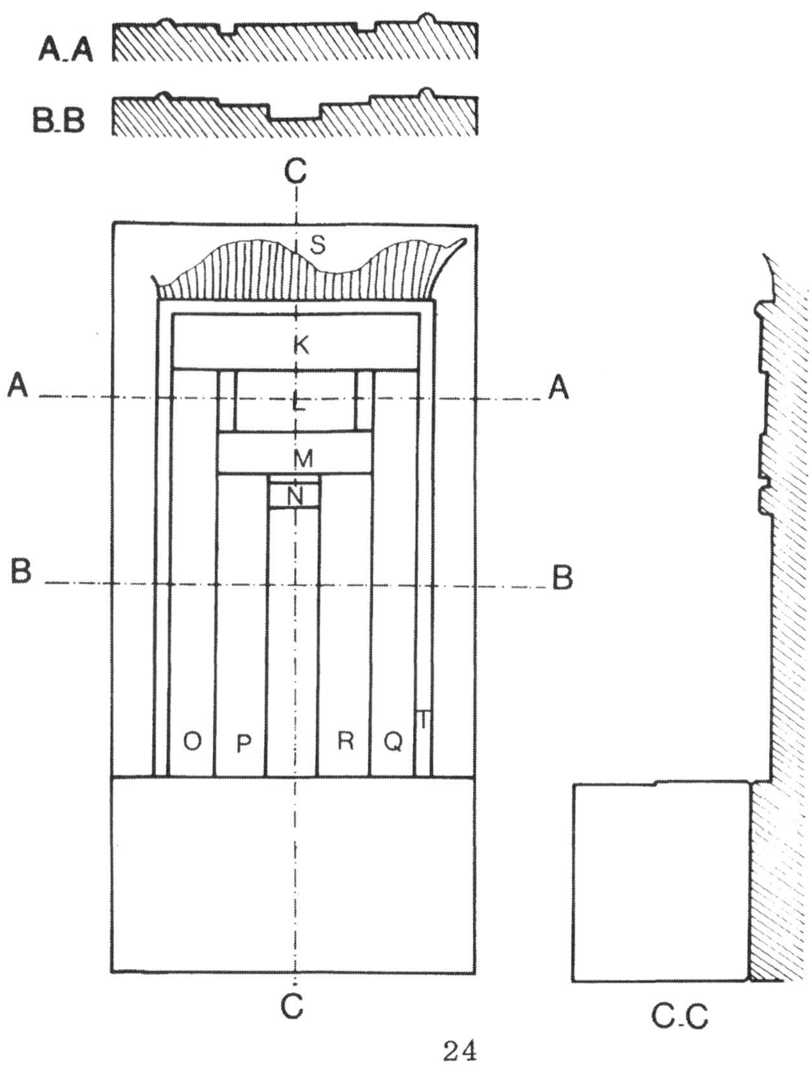

The table of offerings at the foot of the stela was made from one block of limestone measuring 1.05 x 50 x 47 metres. The surface is pitted. This offering table depicts a *ḥtp*-sign in relief, this being the right way round to the dead man when he emerges from the door, and consequently upside-down to a person standing before the false-door. (8 on plan, p. 4 above).

Inscriptions on the false-door: (pl. 9; Fig. 7).

N : The drum:

ḥꜣty-ꜥ Rꜥ-wr

The Count Rēꜥ-wer

L : The panel:

The deceased is represented as a seated figure; before him, his name has been scratched out. Read "Rēꜥ-wer".

K : Upper lintel:

ḥtp di nsw ḥtp di ꞌInpw tpy ḏw.f pr (n.f) ḫrw t ḥnḳt rꜥ nb[42] *(mry nṯr*[43] *) Rꜥ-wr.*

A boon which the king gives, and a boon which Anubis gives, who resides over his mountain, that invocation offerings may come forth (for him) consisting of bread and beer every day (the one beloved of the god) Rēꜥ-wer.

M : Lower lintel:

imꜣḫw ḫr nṯr ꜥꜣ imy-r šmꜥ Rꜥ-wr

Honoured by the great god, overseer of Upper Egypt Rēꜥ-wer.

O : *ḥtp di Wsir nb Ḏdw ḫp.f r imntt ḫr nṯr ꜥꜣ mry nṯr Rꜥ-wr.*[44]

A boon which Osiris Lord of Busiris gives, that he may go to the west with the great god, the one beloved of the god Rēꜥ-wer.

Q : *ḥtp di ꞌInpw imy wt ḫp.f m ḥtp r s(m)t imntt mry nṯr*[45] *Rꜥ wr.*

A boon which Anubis who is in the bandage gives, that he may go in peace to the western desert, the one beloved of the god Rēꜥ-wer.

P : *ỉmꜣḫw ḫr nṯrw šmꜥ ḫry-ḥb mry nṯr* [46] *Rꜥ-wr.*

The one honoured by the gods of Upper Egypt, the lector priest, beloved of the god Rēꜥ-wer.

R : *ỉmꜣḫw ḫr nṯr tꜣyty sꜣb ṯꜣty mry nṯr* [47] *Rꜥ-wr.*

The one honoured by the god, the shrouded one, judge, and vizier, beloved of the god Rēꜥ-wer.

Thus the original and altered readings starting from the left (O) are as follows:

	Original	Altered
O	*ḫr nṯr ꜥꜣ (ḥꜣty-ꜥ) Rꜥ-wr*	... *ḫr nṯr ꜥꜣ (mry nṯr) Rꜥ-wr*
P	*ḫr nṯrw šmꜥw (smr wꜥty) Rꜥ-wr*	... *ḫr nṯrw šmꜥ (ḫry ḥb mry nṯr) Rꜥ-wr*
R	*ḫr nṯr tꜣyty sꜣb ṯꜣty (ḥꜣty-ꜥ) Rꜥ-wr*	... *tꜣyty sꜣb ṯꜣty (mry nṯr) Rꜥ-wr*
Q	*r smt ỉmntt (sḏꜣwty bỉty) Rꜥ-wr*	... *r smt ỉmntt (mry nṯr) Rꜥ-wr*

An alteration has also been made in the figure of the deceased at the bottom of the jamb (R), where the artist has doubled the figure. In considering the interpretation of these facts, it is to be noted that:

i) There is no evidence of the name *Rꜥ-wr* being carved over any other name in these four columns: it is clearly original as in the other inscriptions (K,N) on the false door.

ii) The mutilation of the name *Rꜥ-wr* is here similar to that in the rest of the tomb; there is no sign of its being replaced by any other name; and the technique of the mutilation is different from that attempted on the titles.

iii) The titles replaced by *mry-nṯr* in columns O, P, R and Q, namely *ḥꜣty-ꜥ, smr wꜥty, ḥꜣty-ꜥ, sḏꜣwty-bỉty*, are all titles of Rēꜥ-wer which appear elsewhere in the tomb (north false-door, entrance door jambs), and on the statues recorded by Gunn (Gunn MSS XV-8, Notebook, IX, nos. 1,2), see below, p. 35.

iv) The title *mry-nṯr* is part of Rēꜥ-wer's full titulary, since it also appears on the jambs of the entrance to the tomb, where it has been mutilated like Rēꜥ-wer's name, and on the south false door, where it is certainly part of the original inscription.

v) Thus the conclusion must be that the replacement of other titles by *mry-nṯr* on the north false door is not due to a usurpation; both *mry-nṯr* and the titles it replaced are part of Rēʿ-wer's full titulary. The explanation of the replacements here must remain uncertain. It seems probable that the title *mry-nṯr* was especially important to Rēʿ-wer, because everywhere he writes it next to his name. As the northern stela is in yellow limestone, unlike the white limestone of other parts of the tomb, it seems possible that this false door was carved rather earlier than the other parts of the tomb, before Rēʿ-wer was granted the title *mry nṯr*. If so, he might well have ordered it to be carved on the stela in place of certain of his other titles which appear elsewhere. The title *mry-nṯr* appears also in the titulary of *Ḫwy*, the father of the *t3yty s3b ṯ3ty Ḏʿw* of Abydos, whose two sisters, both called *ʿnḫ.n.s-Mry-rʿ*, were queens of Pepy I, and mothers of Mernerēʿ and Pepy II respectively; *Ḫwy* otherwise bears only the honorific titles *iry-pʿt ḥ3ty-ʿ im3ḫw ḫr nṯr ʿ3* in this inscription (Sethe, Urkunden des Alten Reichs I, Leipzig, 1933, p. 119, l.2). Possibly *Ḫwy* had not held high office himself, but derived his importance from that of his son *Ḏʿw* and his two queenly daughters; thus it may be that the title *mry nṯr* is a special honorific. Otherwise, I have not succeeded in finding other examples of the use of *mry nṯr* in the Old Kingdom, though it is of course commonly used in association with the priestly title *it-nṯr* in the New Kingdom (Wb. II.101,3; A.H. Gardiner, Ancient Egyptian Onomastica, Oxford, 1947, I, 50 ff., where he discusses the use of *it-nṯr* and *mry-nṯr* by persons standing in the relation of father or father-in-law to the reigning king, as did *Ḏʿw*). This comparison suggests speculations concerning the reasons for Rēʿ-wer's favour with the king and his possible relation to him, which cannot be substantiated.

F. Jambs of the north false-door (pl. 8, nos. 7,9).

On both sides of the northern false-door are incised seven horizontal lines giving the names of the seven sacred oils. There are seven jars, all  except the fourth, which is : against them at the left of each is written the name of the contents.

The southern jamb (pl. 8, no. 7) (reading from the top).

1-2. The first two sacred oils are missing.

3. *sfṯ* : A sacred oil.

4. *nḫnm* : A sacred oil.

5. *tw3tw* : A sacred oil.

6. *ḥ3tt ʿš* : Finest oil of *ʿš*-wood.

7. *ḥ3tt tḥnw* : Finest Libyan oil.

On the left jamb (south) of this false-door, opposite the horizontal lines numbered 3-4, was originally carved a figure of a man carrying a tray of fruit and vegetables on his right shoulder, and with papyrus stems hanging from his right elbow. This block was therefore reused from another tomb.

The northern jamb (pl. 8, no. 9).

1. *sṯ-ḥb* : A sacred oil. The name of this, the first of the group of seven sacred oils, means "the perfume of the festival", which is clear from the two elements *sṯ* "perfume" and *ḥb* "festival". The *sṯ-ḥb* was not only used for personal anointing, it was also employed for perfuming the temples.[48] Maspero also considered *sṯ-ḥb* to have been a perfume, and says that its basis was an oil mixed with some aromatic substance which rendered it thick like ointment.[49]

2. *ḥknw* : A sacred oil.

3. *sfṯ* : A sacred oil.

4. *nẖnm* : A sacred oil.

5. *twꜣwt* : A sacred oil.

6. *ḥꜣtt ꜥš* : Finest oil of *ꜥš*-wood.

7. *ḥꜣtt tḥnw* : Finest Libyan oil.

6. The North wall (pl. 10, Fig. 8).

The north wall measures 1.26 metres in length and 1.52 metres in height, and consists of three courses (Fig. 8). The scene occupying this wall is common in the Old Kingdom mastabas on the walls of the false-door rooms, showing bearers bringing offerings to the deceased. The scene consists of four registers; the upper register is missing as usual in this monument. The principal figure is as is customary at the west end of the wall nearest the stela or the false-door.

The workmanship of the scene varies: the deceased was represented in raised relief, but the offering-bearers are in outline. The owner of the tomb, Rēꜥ-wer, is represented on this wall as a standing figure (on the left side of the wall), holding a long straight staff in his left hand, and a *sḫm* sceptre with an open papyrus head in the right hand. He is also wearing a *wsḫ* collar and bracelets, and a flaring kilt reaching to the knees; it is formed of a single piece of cloth wrapped round the body, draped high at the back and low at the front, and tied at the waist. He has a leopard skin over his shoulder. The skin is tied on the left shoulder, though the method of fastening is not shown, and the cords of the tie fall on each side of his left shoulder. The claws of the leopard skin fall over Rēꜥ-wer's left arm with the right shoulder bare. The tail is brought across both his thighs and hangs straight down between his legs.

The inscription in front of the standing figure of the deceased is broken in some parts. The remains of the vertical line reads as follows:

....(ỉ)nnt n.f sic *ḥwt.f m niwt.f (nt*[50] *tꜣ) mḥw šmꜥ prt ḫrw t ḥnḳt n.f ỉm.*

..... which are brought to him (from) his estates, and from his towns (of) Lower and Upper Egypt, that invocation offerings of bread and beer may come forth to him there.

Before the standing figure of the deceased there are four registers occupying the wall; the movement of the figures is to the west in the direction of the north false-door. All the men who follow are dressed alike in short kilts tied at the waist, but with no diagonal curved line showing the edge of the fabric where it is wrapped across the body. They wear short wigs. None of the offering-bearers is named.

In the topmost register remains of offerings can be seen: baskets, jars, offering-tables, and bread. In the second register, there are four offering-bearers: the first carries a tray of meat and loaves on his right shoulder, then comes a man carrying on his right shoulder a covered dish. Papyrus stems hang from his right arm, and across his left arm he holds papyrus stalks and a jar. The third carries a tray of bread and cakes and lotus buds on his right shoulder, and holds a bird by its wings in his left hand. The last figure is heavily laden. On his right shoulder he carries a tray laden with loaves and cakes, with a basket hanging from his right arm; on his left shoulder he carries a tray of loaves and bread; papyrus stems hang from his left elbow and a jar hangs from his left wrist; at his side walks a calf.

In the third register there are four men carrying offerings; most of these figures are pitted. The remains of the offerings are as follows: The first offering-bearer carries a large bundle of papyrus stems which hangs from his right arm. The second carries on his right shoulder a tray laden with bread, loaves and papyrus stems. The third carries a covered dish on his right shoulder, lotus blossoms and buds in his left hand(?), and lotus blossoms hang from his left arm. The last figure holds papyrus stalks across his right arm and a big jar in his right hand. A lotus blossom hangs from his left arm.

In the lowest register four men carry the choicest haunches of beef from the sacrificial victim to the owner of the tomb. They carry them by crooking their right arms under the thigh of the beast and holding the hoof with their left hands.

The surface of this wall is in a bad state of preservation.

7. The East wall (pl. 11; 12; 13; 14; pl. 20B; Fig. 9).

Fig. 8: Masonry of North wall

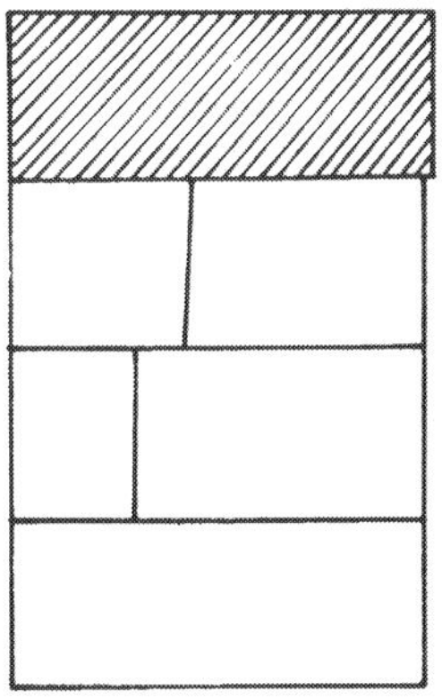

Fig. 9: Masonry of East wall

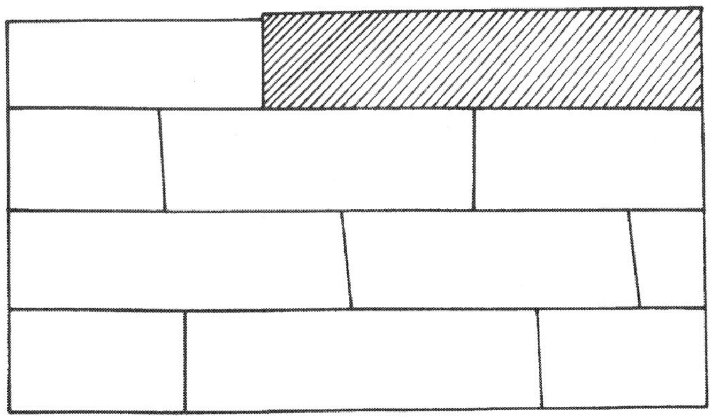

Scale 1:20. Top courses reconstructed.

The east wall is the longest wall in the tomb: it measures 3.57 metres in length, and 2.00 metres in height. This wall consists of four courses, the most complete section being in the north-east corner. The fourth course has disappeared except for the last block at the north end, a single limestone block measuring 1.33 x 0.44 metres. The fourth course has now been restored by using small blocks of local white limestone to bring the wall up to the original height of the tomb (Fig. 9; 11 on plan, p. 4 above). There are four registers occupying this wall. The remains of the first register (from the top), which is partially destroyed, consist of double rows of offerings of different kinds of food: cakes, fruits, joints of meat, vases in many shapes, birds, loaves, bunches of onions, lettuces and jars, a head of sacrificial ox, many trays laden with offerings, all piled up in confusion (pl. 14). At the entrance of the tomb only the remains of the lower part of the first register can still be seen.

In the second register, which measures 23 cm. in height, there are 29 offering bearers walking in procession northwards. They are part of the same procession which extends along the north and west walls walks to the northern false-door. All the men who follow are dressed virtually alike, in short wigs and short kilts, but while most of the kilts show the edge of the material as a diagonal carved line, in some cases this is omitted. They carry various offerings. In this register, none of the offering-bearers is named. The first from the left (pl. 13) holds papyrus stalks with lotuses in his right hand; on his left shoulder he carries a covered jar, and papyrus buds hang from his left elbow. The second is heavily laden: on his right shoulder he holds an *usekh*-

basket containing loaves, and there is a jar hanging from his right elbow. Across his chest, in his left hand he holds a long object which may represent papyrus stalks with their ends cut off, [51] and there is a broad seed basket hanging from his left elbow. The third carries a tray laden with loaves and vegetables on his right shoulder and a jar hangs from his right elbow; in his left hand he holds a jar. The fourth is heavily laden. On one shoulder he has a tray of loaves, vegetables and vases, with an open papyrus flower over his arm; in the other hand, which is placed across his chest, he carries another tray, and a vase is hanging from his elbow. The fifth is carrying a tray of loaves and vases on his right shoulder, and there is an open papyrus flower hanging over his arm; in his right hand he is carrying a live bird by its wings across his chest. The next is laden with a tray of loaves and vases on the right shoulder, with papyrus blooms over his elbow, and in the other hand, which is stretched down his side, he holds a live bird. The seventh is laden with a covered dish and holds a bundle of papyrus or perhaps pieces of wood(?) across his chest, while a vase with a handle hangs from his arm. Then comes a man carrying a tray full of meat(?) and loaves on his right shoulder and there are papyrus buds hanging from his right arm. He holds another round tray across his chest with his left hand, where there is an open papyrus blossom and buds also hanging. The next has a tray laden with loaves and meat and lotuses hanging from the elbow; in his left hand he is holding two trussed geese. Then comes a man carrying a tray with loaves on his right shoulder and a basket with a handle; in his left hand he holds a bird by its wings. The eleventh carries a tray laden with loaves and vegetables on his right shoulder and a basket with a handle over his right arm; across his chest in his left hand he holds papyrus stalks and a vase hangs from his left elbow. Then comes a man carrying a tray laden with bread and a basket with a handle, and a jar hangs from his left hand. The next is heavily laden with two trays on his shoulders with cakes and loaves, and there is a basket hanging from his right arm, and a papyrus stem with buds is draped from the other arm. The next carries papyrus stalks and lotus flowers across his right arm. In his left arm which is stretched at his side he holds a lotus flower.

Following him there is a man carrying a tray with loaves and vegetables and a basket with a handle over his right arm, and in the other hand, placed across his chest, he holds a live bird by its wings. The next carries the least, his offering consisting of a bundle of papyrus stalks, and a goose held in his left hand by its wings. The seventeenth carries a tray laden with vases and vegetables and there are lotus buds hanging from his right elbow. Across his chest, in his left hand, is a long object, possibly a papyrus roll or piece of wood(?), and a basket with a handle hanging from his arm. The eighteenth carries a young calf across his shoulders, and holds two of its legs in each hand. This right arm is around the animal's neck, and its front legs are stretched out trying to leap to freedom. Stems of papyrus hang from his left arm. The nineteenth carries a bird by its wings with his right arm across his chest and a water jar with a handle hanging from the right elbow. A lotus blossom and a bud are in his left hand. There is a roll of papyrus or a piece of wood across his back. The twentieth is laden with a tray of loaves and vegetables over his right shoulder and there is a basket hanging from his right elbow. On his left arm he carries a covered dish and a jar with a handle. The next man carries a live bird firmly by its beak and legs, and a lotus flower and buds hang from his right arm. The next carries a covered dish on his right shoulder and a basket with a handle; and a bird held by the wings in the other hand. The next carries a tray with vases, and something resembling a piece of cloth(?) hangs across his right elbow, though it may in fact be only a faulty representation of a lotus flower. Across his left arm he holds papyrus stalks. The twenty-fourth has a basket hanging from his elbow, a tray of loaves and vegetables, and a lotus flower in his left hand, while his right hand hangs at his side. The next carries a tray of loaves and vases on his right shoulder and holds a duck by its wings in his left arm. The twenty-sixth (badly damaged) carries a tray of loaves and vases, a basket hangs from his right elbow, and there is probably another tray in his left arm(?) with a water jar hanging from his left elbow. This jar has a decoration of horizontal lines, like that held by the eighth bearer in the second register. Here, however, there is an added vertical line feature, not understood, perhaps signifying that there are two jars. Another man follows, carrying a bird firmly by the beak and legs, with lotus blossoms and buds over his left arm. On the other arm he holds a jar with a handle. The twenty-eighth carries a tray of covered vases and lotus flowers hanging from his right shoulder, and lotus blossoms grasped within his left arm. He is followed by the last figure in this procession, heavily laden with a tray on which is a covered vase and loaves and papyrus stems hanging from his elbow. Across his chest in his left hand he holds a long object, perhaps papyrus stems or a piece of wood(?), and a water-jar hangs from his left wrist.

In the third register which measures 23 cms. in height, there are 29 figures, the same number as in the second register, bringing the same offerings to the tomb owner. They are laden with different kinds of jars, vases, trays full of loaves and vegetables and covered dishes, birds, geese, lotus blossoms and buds and papyrus stems. In this register none of the offering-bearers is named, and all are dressed alike in short wigs and short kilts. In the composition of this scene, the offerings represented are thus relatively limited in type: yet no single offering bearer holds precisely the same offerings in the same position. It does not seem possible to establish a regular order in which the offerings alternate, either between individual figures or registers, though there is a tendency for certain offerings, like birds and seed-baskets, to occur in places with alternate figures; elsewhere they are further apart or even held by successive figures. The only offering to occur but once is the calf on the shoulders of figure eighteen of register two. Here then, the artist shows considerable skill in disposing his relatively limited repertoire.

The lowest register (the fourth) measuring 23 cms. in height, is given up, as is the general rule, to a scene of sacrifice. The butchers and their assistants slaughter and dismember the animals. The group of men are varied and the position of the principal operator is slightly different. In the first group (from the left) there are two butchers and the ox lying on the ground. They cut and open the ox and remove the foreleg, while another butcher carries away a haunch of meat on his shoulder. Above the victim and between the two butchers one of them says to his companion: *sfṯ wn* "cut, hurry up!". The man who carries the *ḫpš*-foreleg is badly damaged. In the second group the foreleg of the victim is being removed by two butchers, while another man of the group holds the cord which ties the victim firmly. Another figure carries away a bowl of blood(?) on his left shoulder with a piece of meat or a cloth in his right hand. In other tombs, by the side of the victim a boy kneeling on one knee is often depicted holding a large bowl to catch the blood.[52] In the third group, the animal has been skinned: the last figure in that group is holding the leg of the victim in his arms. The next carries the *ḫpš* on his right shoulder and the heart of the victim in his left hand; others are busy cutting up other parts of the victim.

In the fourth group which follows the animal has been thrown on the ground and is being tied with the cord: two of the butcher's assistants hold firmly on to the cord from the sides of the ox, while the butcher (the third member of the group) sharpens his knife. In the next group of butchers one of the members carries away a haunch of meat, another takes out the heart in his left hand, while the third is wielding his knife.

In the sixth group the butchers are cutting off the front leg of the ox, and the third member of the group is leaving them carrying a bowl of the blood of the animal on his left shoulder and holding a piece of meat in his right hand.

The seventh group of butchers in this scene consists of four figures. Three of them are occupied with the victim, two in cutting off the foreleg, and another in skinning the animal, while the other member of the group carries the front leg over his right shoulder and the heart in his left hand.

In the last group, the ox is lying on the ground firmly tied by a cord, the latter being held by one of the butcher's assistants, while the front leg of the victim is being cut off by two men.

In one figure in this slaughtering scene the artist has captured an aspect of the body almost in true profile, but the device of turning over the shoulder is still common.

As I have mentioned, all the offering bearers who follow in these processions are dressed virtually alike, in short kilts, but the sculptor has not carved the upper horizontal edge of the material of the kilt nor its diagonal edge (as in the figures number 1-5-9-12-13 in the second register and those numbered 4-7-9-12-22-27 in the third register), but he nevertheless carved the tie at the waist. In some cases he did not join the lines of the offerings, as the vertical line of the covered jar on the left shoulder and the basket which hangs from the right elbow of the figure numbered 13 in the second register, and the offerings which the last three figures in this register are carrying. Sometimes, the sculptor had not enough skill either in holding or in controlling the chisel, which he used in carving the scenes, as can be seen in the figures numbers 8-19-24-26 in the third register, and in the seventh group of butchers.

CHAPTER IV

Statues and blocks found in and around the tomb of Rēʿ-wer

1. Statue 1 of Rēʿ-wer  Figure of a man in a loincloth, seated, with hands on knees, on cubical seat with projection under feet.[53]

a.	Material	:	mottled granite.
b.	Dimensions	:	original height about 1.05 m.
c.	Work	:	fair.
d.	Preservation	:	head lost, hands damaged.
e.	Colour	:	none.
f.	Technique	:	incised.

Texts

A. Before the feet:

Smr wʿty, ỉmy-r šmʿ, mry nṯr Rʿ-wr.

Sole Companion, Overseer of Upper Egypt, beloved of the god Rēʿ-wer.

B. To left[54] of feet:

ỉry-pʿt, mry nṯr Rʿ-wr.[55]

Hereditary prince, beloved of the god Rēʿ-wer.

C. To right of feet:

ỉry-pʿt, mry nṯr Rʿ-wr.

Hereditary prince, beloved of the god Rēʿ-wer.

D. Down middle of left side of seat:

iry-pʿt, imy-r šmʿ, imꜣḫw mry nṯr Rʿ-wr.

Hereditary prince, overseer of Upper Egypt, honoured one, beloved of the god Rēʿ-wer.

E. Down middle of right side of seat:

tꜣyty sꜣb ṯꜣty, imy-r Šmʿ[56] sic *imꜣḫ(w) mry nṯr Rʿ-wr.*

The shrouded one, judge and vizier, overseer of Upper Egypt, honoured one, beloved of the god Rēʿ-wer.

F. Down the back:

imꜣḫw ḫr nṯr ʿꜣ, iry-pʿt tꜣyty sꜣb ṯꜣty, imy-r šmʿ, mry nṯr Rʿ-wr.

The one honoured of the great god, the hereditary prince, the shrouded one, judge and vizier, overseer of Upper Egypt, beloved of the god Rēʿ-wer.

2. <u>Statue 2 of Rēʿ-wer,</u>  similar to the preceding.

Height : 1.30 m.

Preservation: The part above the waist is lost.

<u>Texts</u>

A. Before the feet:

Smr wʿty, imy-r šmʿ, mry nṯr Rʿ-wr.

The sole companion, Overseer of Upper Egypt, beloved of the god Rēʿ-wer.

B. To left of feet:

ḥꜣty-ʿ, mry nṯr Rʿ-wr.

The Count, beloved of the god Rēʿ-wer.

C. To right of feet:

ḥꜣty-ꜥ, mry nṯr Rꜥ-wr.

The Count, beloved of the god Rēꜥ-wer.

D. Down middle of left side of seat:

ṯꜣyty sꜣb ṯꜣty, ỉmy-r šmꜥ ỉmꜣḫw mry nṯr Rꜥ-wr.

The shrouded one, judge and the vizier, overseer of Upper Egypt, the one honoured, beloved of the god Rēꜥ-wer.

E. Down middle of right side of seat:

ṯꜣyty sꜣb ṯꜣty, ỉmy-r šmꜥ, ỉmꜣḫw mry nṯr Rꜥ-wr.

The shrouded one, judge and vizier, overseer of Upper Egypt, the one honoured, beloved of the god Rēꜥ-wer.

F. Down the back:

(ỉmꜣḫw) ḫr nṯr ꜥꜣ, ỉry-pꜥt, ḥꜣty-ꜥ ṯꜣyty (sꜣb ṯꜣty), ỉmy-r šmꜥ mry nṯr Rꜥ-wr.

(The one honoured) by the great god, the hereditary prince, the Count, the shrouded one (judge and vizier) overseer of Upper Egypt, beloved of the god Rēꜥ-wer.

3. Inscribed blocks found in and around the tomb.

A. Discovered in the recent excavations

i) Limestone sarcophagus (see pl. 18, no. 1).

A rectangular sarcophagus was found buried in the debris to the south of the temenos wall of the tomb. It measures 2.20 x 0.80 x 0.40 metres and consists of rough blocks of local limestone put together and plastered with gypsum, five blocks forming the base, two blocks on the south side, one block on the north side and one block at the east end. This last is a part of the lid. Inside was found the burial of a man in a very bad state of preservation with only the skull remaining. He was lying on his back, the head to the east. There were no objects with the burial, and its date must remain uncertain. These blocks were moved to the side of the tomb to enable the excavation to continue. It seems that many burials were buried in these heaps of debris: traces of them can be seen in the debris sections waiting to come to light. The stratification of these burials shows clearly that they must postdate the destruction of the Teti pyramid temple.

On the other hand, they are clearly at a lower level than the New Kingdom tomb chapels in the area.[57] As Quibell found Middle Kingdom burials to the south-west, and south of the ritual pyramid, it seems possible that they may be of about that date.[58]

ii) Scarab (see pl. 18, no. 2).

A scarab of blue glazed steatite was found in the debris on the south side of the tomb, inscribed *ḥkꜣ tꜣwy* "ruler of the Two Lands". The scarab shows divisions between the head, the elytra and the prothorax, but is cut in a very rudimentary manner, some of the lines being incomplete. The clypeus is only notionally shown, and there are no nicks on the wing cases. The profile of the scarab is very flat; it is round-ended with straight lines narrowing towards the head. The legs are not shown. On the base there is a plain border, and the inscription is very deeply incised. The form and details of the scarab suggest that it is of Second Intermediate Period date.

iii) Small offering-tables (pl. 15).

It is impossible to say whether these small offering-tables belonged to the tomb; they were found in the debris outside the entrance to the tomb.

No. 1 (pl. 15, no. 1) shows a *ḥtp*-sign and a tank; it measures 73 x 25 x 8 cms.

No. 2 (pl. 15, no. 2) shows a loaf in a trough between two *ḥs*-jars, with two rectangular and two round depressions above. It measures 63 x 40 x 10 cms.

No. 3 (pl. 15, no. 3) shows the loaf of the *ḥtp* sign between two rectangular tanks. It measures 18 x 10 x 7 cms.

The dates are uncertain, though all may belong to the Old Kingdom.

Fragments found in a small pit west of the tomb of Rēʿ-wer.

iv) Reg. No. 17290 (pl. 16, no. 4). This fragment was previously seen and recorded by Battiscombe Gunn (see Gunn MSS XIX, 39). Fragment, upper part of a false-door dedicated to *ppi-ḥꜣ-išˇtf*. Remains of three vertical lines in deeply inscribed hieroglyphs, reads from left to right.

a. ....*imy-r šnʿ Ppi-ḥꜣ-ištf*.[59]

....overseer of the workshops *Ppi-ḥꜣ-ištf*.

b. ....*ḥ3.išṯf*. (The end of the cartouche only of the name *ppi* is preserved). Here the deceased is represented as a standing figure holding the long straight staff in his right hand, and the *ḫrp* sceptre in his left hand, wearing the flaring kilt and a long wig.

c. ....*ḥ3.išṯf*.

....*ḥ3.išṯf*. He is represented standing with his arms stretched at his side. This fragment is of Old Kingdom date, Sixth-Eighth Dynasty.

v) Reg. No. 17289 (pl. 16, no. 5), measures 55 x 45 cms. The left lower part of a false-door of white limestone belongs to *ipi-m-s3-f*. It is inscribed in three vertical lines, reading from right to left:

a. ....*Wsir Ipi-(m-s3.f)*.

....the Osiris Ipi-em-sa-ef.

b. ....*m is.t(?)ḥr sgri m ḥwt wrt Ipi-(m-s3.f)*.

....in the palace of the master of silence(?), in the great palace Ipi-(em-sa-ef).

At the bottom of the left column the deceased is shown standing facing right, raising his hands in adoration. He wears a flaring kilt, a *wsḫ*-collar and a long wig. His legs are missing; in the centre column, only a fragment of the wig and shoulder of a similar figure are preserved.

c. ....*(m)is.f n ḫr-nṯr*[60] *im3ḫ Ipi-m-s3.f*.[61]

....(in) his tomb of the necropolis, the revered one Ipi-em-sa-ef. This fragment is of Old Kingdom date, probably Fifth-Sixth Dynasty.

vi) Reg. no. 17291 (pl. 17, no. 6). This fragment was previously seen and recorded by Battiscombe Gunn (see Gunn MSS XIX, 41). It measures 18 x 10 x 7 cms. A part of a long block of white limestone, inscribed in three vertical lines. Only traces of the third line can be seen.

a. *(i3w?) n.k ḥp ꜥnḫ wḥm n Ptḥ* ....

"praise" to you, O living Apis, the herald of *Ptḥ* ...

b. *dỉ.f ḥtpw ḏfw ....*

May he give good offerings .....

c. *Ws(ỉr) ỉmy-r pr n nb tꜣwy ....*

The Osiris, the steward of Lord of the two lands ....

To the left of the inscriptions, the left shoulder of a man can be seen. This fragment most probably belongs to the New Kingdom.

vii) Reg. no. 17292 (pl. 17, no. 7). This fragment was previously seen and recorded by Battiscombe Gunn (see Gunn MSS, XIX, 40). It measures 25 x 19 - 11 x 7 cms.

A rectangular block of white limestone, probably from the base of a statue, inscribed on two sides, in incised hieroglyphs, reads:

Wp(wty)-nsw r ḫꜣst nb(t) r[62]...

The envoy of the king to all foreign lands ....

On the right side of the block the title *ḥry ssmwt* "overseer of horses" is preserved. This fragment is certainly of the New Kingdom, most probably late Eighteenth-Nineteenth Dynasty.

viii) Fragment of limestone cavetto cornice, showing the usual round-topped vertical panels in incised work, every third being coloured red. Torus moulding in relief, and horizontal line of incised hieroglyphs, reading from right to left:

.....*tp(y) ḏw.f pr-ḫrw tʾ ḥnḳt ...*

.....(May Anubis who is) on his mountain (give) invocation offerings consisting of bread and beer.

The date of this fragment is uncertain.

B. Recorded by Battiscombe Gunn

The following blocks, recorded in Gunn's manuscript notebook no. XIX, 39-42, are published here. They have not been located at Saqqara.

i) Gunn MSS XIX,39. (Fig. 10).

Left hand end of lintel, measures 27 x 43 x 11 cms. Inscribed:

.... *iꜣw(t) nfr(t)* .... *ḫ*

.... a good old age .....

sḥd sẖt ꜣbd[63]

The deptuy of weavers Abed

ḥmt.f ꜥIni[64]

His wife Ini

Fig. 10: Left hand edge of lintel.

ii) Gunn MSS XIX,40. (Fig. 11).

Fragment of lintel, 31 x 22 (now) x 21 has:

.k wsḫt

... the broad hall.

Fig. 11: Fragment of lintel.

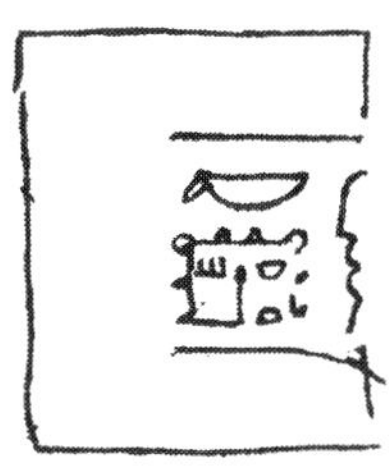

Fig. 12: Upper part of false-door.

iii) Upper part of false door, 37 (now) x 70 x 15: (Fig. 12)

<u>Upper lintel</u>:

ḥtp dỉ nsw ḥtp dỉ 'Inpw prt ḫrw t ḥnḳt nt [sic] *Ḥt-Ḥr ḥm nṯr grgỉ.*

"A boon which the king gives, a boon which Anubis gives, that there may be made invocation offerings consisting of bread and beer for the priestess of Hathor Gregy."

<u>Outer left jamb</u>:

prt ḫrw t ḥnḳt nt [sic] *rḫt nswt*

"An invocation offering consisting of bread and beer of/for the king's acquaintance ...."

<u>Outer right jamb</u>:

prt ḫrw t ḥnḳt nt [sic]

"An invocation offering consisting of bread and beer of/for ..

iv) Gunn MSS XIX,41. (Fig. 13).

Fragment of New Kingdom, has on cornice:

Wsỉr sš šꜥ.t-nsw Rꜥ-mss....

Osiris the scribe of the royal documents Ramesses

Fig. 13: Fragment of New Kingdom inscription.

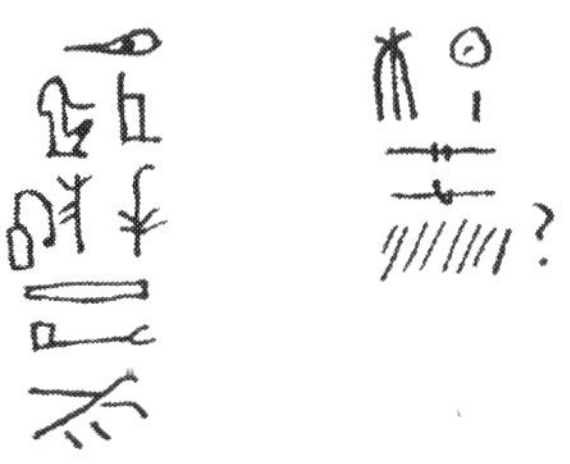

v) Gunn MSS XIX,41. (Fig. 14).

Fragment from south of the little pyramid inscribed:

a. *Tm Ḥr Ḫprỉ dỉ.f ʿnḫ bꜣ*

Atum-Horus-Khepri, may he cause the soul of ..... to live

b. ... *n Wsỉr ṯꜣy ḫw' ḥr wnmw nsw sš mꜣʿ* [65]

... to the Osiris, the fan-bearer on the right of the king, the true royal scribe.......

Fig. 14: Fragment from south of the little pyramid.

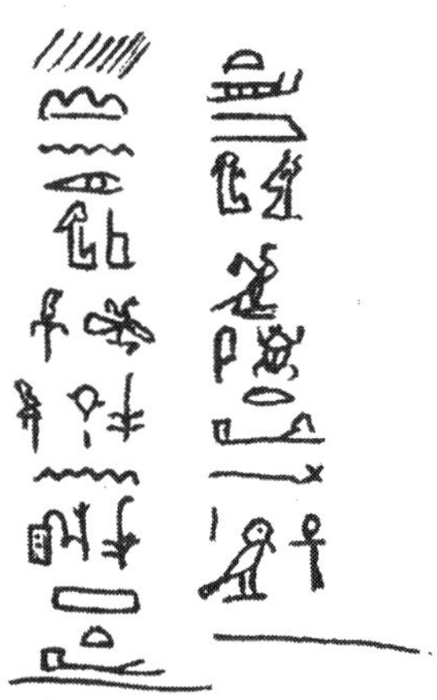

Fig. 15: Fragment north east of the little pyramid.

vi) Gunn MSS XIX,42.

Fragment inscribed in two vertical lines: (Fig. 15).

a. *(nb).w(?) nḥḥ n kꜣ n Wsỉr ṯꜣy ḫw ḥr wnmy nsw*

(All) eternity to the soul of Osiris, the fan-bearer on the right of the king ....

b. *(Ḥr)(?) n kꜣ n Wsỉr ṯꜣy-ḫw ḥr wnmy nsw n ḥm-nṯr*

(Horus)? to the Soul (*kꜣ*) of Osiris, the fan-bearer on the right of the king, the prophet(?).......

CHAPTER V

Rēʿ-wer and his tomb

1. The dating of the tomb

a. The tomb of Rēʿ-wer contains no biographical text of the kind that would enable us to determine its date, nor is there any royal cartouche present in the tomb. We have thus to depend on indirect evidence for the dating of the tomb.

b. The situation of the tomb at the south-east corner of the Mortuary Temple of King Teti outside its perimeter wall suggests that its construction is not likely to have begun before the Mortuary Temple was completed. This was presumably near the end of Teti's reign.

c. At the north-east corner of the Mortuary Temple, outside its perimeter wall, lies the *mastaba* of Khentika Ikhekhi. While its position does not exactly correspond to that of Rēʿ-wer, in that it lies outside the line of the north perimeter wall of the Mortuary Temple and its greatest length is from E. to W., it is broadly analogous. Khentika Ikhekhi was officially attached to the pyramids of both Teti and Pepi I (of the Sixth Dynasty),[66] and therefore cannot have been buried until at least the end of the reign of Pepi I. This may help to indicate the date of the tomb of Rēʿ-wer, for though no further excavation has yet been made to the east, it seems logical that the *mastabas* nearest to the perimeter wall of the Mortuary Temple should be the earliest.

d. The style and workmanship of the reliefs and scenes of Rēʿ-wer are perhaps most closely paralleled by that of the chambers dedicated to Mereruka's son at the north end of his great *mastaba* in the street of tombs immediately to the north of the Teti Pyramid.[67] These *mastabas* were presumably the earliest constructed in the necropolis, and Mereruka himself served Teti. His son's chambers were probably decorated in the time of Pepi I.

e. Porter and Moss assign the tomb of Rēʿ-wer to the late Sixth Dynasty.[68] While this date is certainly possible, the considerations of location and style given above suggest to me that the construction and decoration of the tomb is more likely to have taken place in the reign of Pepi I than in those of Mernerēʿ or Pepi II.

2. The official position and personality of Rēʿ-wer.

Rēʿ-wer held the title *ṯȝyty sȝb ṯȝty*, which has been conventionally translated "Vizier" in this work. As has been noted above,[69] so many officials held this title at this time that it has been reasonably suggested that it had become an honorific appellation borne by men who did not officiate in practice as vizier. The relatively small size of Rēʿ-wer's tomb compared with those of such men as Mereruka, Kagemni, Ankhmahor, Neferseshem Ptah and others buried in the Teti Pyramid Cemeteries may suggest that he was one of these. Nevertheless, the titles *iry-pʿt ḥȝty-ʿ, ṯȝyty sȝb ṯȝty, sḏȝwty bity* and *imy-r šmʿ*, even if they signify status rather than office at this time, must indicate that Rēʿ-wer belonged to the highest group of officials of his time. This also is indicated by the position of his tomb immediately outside the Mortuary Temple, which must be regarded as a favoured one. His actual responsibilities in the royal bureaucracy are not altogether clear from his titles, if he did not in fact officiate as "vizier"; *ẖry ḥbt ḥry tpt* and *Sm* show that he acted, in common with most high officials, in priestly functions. Only *ḫrp šndt nbt* suggests a specialized activity; yet this title is so common in the titularies of men of Rēʿ-wer's rank as to suggest that it is also of an honorific nature. Rēʿ-wer himself laid most stress on his title *mry nṯr;* if *nṯr* in this title refers to the pharaoh, then it is possible that his distinction depended rather directly on the royal favour.

It is thus of interest to emphasize that nowhere in the texts of the tomb does Rēʿ-wer mention a single one of his relatives, nor is he shown in the reliefs with any other person who might be interpreted as a member of his family. This must be accounted a very rare phenomenon in ancient Egypt, and seems to be unparallelled among owners of important tombs of the Sixth Dynasty. Rēʿ-wer's silence concerning his father, mother, and children might be interpreted as an indication that he came from a humble background, which he did not choose to emphasize. His claim to fame would then depend purely on his own favour with the king and presumably on his competence in office. This humble background and lack of means might also help to explain the small size of his tomb. Less easy to explain is Rēʿ-wer's failure to depict or mention a wife and children. It is tempting to assume that he died a bachelor or very early in marriage, but this cannot be certain. It is possible that Rēʿ-wer built his own offering chamber first, but intended to extend the tomb with other chambers to provide cults for his family. However, excavation provided no architectural evidence for such an intention. Moreover, the fact that Rēʿ-wer had himself represented twice before offering tables in the central antithetical composition on the west wall of the tomb, and flanking it erected two false-doors for himself without any representation of his family, seems deliberately intended to emphasize his isolation. There is not even a *kȝ*-priest*(ḥm-kȝ)* shown enacting the funerary-cult, who surely would have been represented had Rēʿ-wer had children. Yet to hold the titles he did he must surely have reached full adulthood. This again raises the question of Rēʿ-wer's true function at court, and of what was the precise significance of the title *mry nṯr* "beloved of the god".

One other monument may perhaps be invoked to suggest an explanation of these puzzling aspects of Rēʿ-wer's personality and position. The erasure of the name of Rēʿ-wer everywhere in his tomb suggests that he was disgraced, though other explanations, such as personal vindictiveness on the part of a powerful enemy, are perhaps tenable. If Rēʿ-wer did in fact hold office as vizier, and, as suggested above, this was during the reign of Pepi I, then he appears to be the only one of the six men[70] who may have been viziers in Pepi I's reign who was so disgraced. As Dr. Málek of the Griffith Institute, Oxford has suggested to me, Rēʿ-wer may then be the vizier whose name has been erased from the famous Dahshur Decree, set up in the time of Pepi I to secure exemptions for the two pyramids of Snefru.[71] The space after the title *tȝyty sȝb ṯȝty* of the vizier where the name was erased is very short, and the vertical writing of Rēʿ-wer's name regularly used in the tomb would fit it better than the names of the other probable viziers of Pepi I's reign.[72] Unfortunately, the other titles of the vizier of the Dahshur Decree have also been erased, with the exception of one partially preserved title which begins with *nsw* ...... "king's .....[73] As no such title occurs in Rēʿ-wer's tomb, this must be accounted as important evidence against the identification. However, it is probably not conclusive, since the title *imi-r sš ʿ nswt*, Overseer of the Scribes of the royal documents, which Goedicke suggests restoring,[74] is so standard a part of the vizier's official titulary that it might have been omitted in his private tomb. As has been stressed above, in his tomb Rēʿ-wer everywhere set the title *mry nṯr* next to his name and after *tȝyty sȝb ṯȝty*, in some instances erasing other titles to put it there.[75] Thus, the fact that *tȝyty sȝb ṯȝty* stood immediately before the name in the Dahshur Decree may be regarded as an argument against the identity of that vizier with Rēʿ-wer, but again an inconclusive one. Disgrace early in his career as vizier might also be used to explain the small size of Rēʿ-wer's tomb in relation to its privileged position near the Mortuary Temple of Teti. His disgrace might also be the reason for his failure to include his family in the scenes, if he intended to add further chambers.[76] Tempting as it is, however, to see Rēʿ-wer as the vizier of the Dahshur Decree, such evidence as survives is negative or inconclusive, and the problem must remain open. If the identity is accepted, the date of Rēʿ-wer's death must have been later than the 21st count of Pepi I, the date of the decree. Goedicke has suggested in JAOS 74 (1954), 88-89, that the *imi-r ḫnty-š pr-ʿȝ Wni* of Abydos was appointed to try the first queen of Pepi I despite his lowly rank (Sethe, Urkunden I, 100-101) because the vizier of the Dahshur Decree had been disgraced, that is after *ḥȝt-sp* 21 of Pepi I; he does not however identify the vizier with Rēʿ-wer. If, however, Rēʿ-wer's title *mry nṯr* is taken to suggest (see above, p. 27) that he was father to a wife of King Pepi, then his disgrace might well have been due to the disgrace of the queen tried by Uni. This might be so, even if the vizier of the Dahshur Decree were not Rēʿ-wer; but it is tempting at least to bring all these events together. The disgrace of Rēʿ-wer and his daughter might then have been the event which brought the family of *Ḫwy* of Abydos to prominence.

THE NOTES

1. For a complete plan of the Mortuary Temple of Teti, with restoration, see J.-Ph. Lauer and J. Leclant, *Mission Archéologique de Saqqarah*, I. *Le Temple haut du complexe funéraire du roi Téti*. (Cairo, 1972), pl. XXXV.

2. T. G. H. James and M. R. Apted, *The mastaba of Khentika called Ikhekhi*, (London, 1953).

3. P. Duell, and others, *The mastaba of Mereruka*, 2 vols. (Chicago, 1938); J. Capart, *Une rue de tombeaux a Saqqarah*, II (Brussels, 1907); F. W. Freiherr von Bissing, *Die Mastaba des Gem-ni-kai*, 2 vols. (Berlin, 1905, 1911).

4. For preliminary report see H. S. Smith and D. G. Jeffreys, *JEA* 64 (1978), 10 f., and *JEA* 65 (1979), 17 f.

5. The tombs in this area are at present being copied and planned by an Egypt Exploration Society expedition under Mr. W. V. Davies, Dr. A. B. Lloyd and Dr. A. J. Spencer, working in conjunction with the Egyptian Antiquities Service represented by Dr. Ali El-Khouli, and also by a mission from the University of Berkeley, California, led by Dr. A. Badawi. For this reason no new plan of this area is published in this volume.

6. J. E. Quibell, *Excavations at Saqqara, 1906-7* (Cairo, 1908), pl. IV. Plate III shows the east side of the small pyramid and the court east of it. The mounds of debris on the right of the plate show that Quibell did not excavate beyond the enclosure wall.

7. C. M. Firth and B. Gunn, *Teti Pyramid Cemeteries,* I (Cairo, 1926), 8.

8. Quibell, op. cit., pl. III.

9. I would like to thank Mr. C. J. Eyre for help with locating and reproducing these records.

10. I am grateful to the authorities of the Griffith Institute, to Dr. Jaromír Málek and Miss Helen Murray for allowing me to consult Gunn's manuscripts, and for permission to publish extracs from them in this work.

11. Two false-doors. Gunn MSS,XIV.53-4 and R.1.3,4,10 (photos and tracings); Notebook, 19.32-8; and two seated headless statues of deceased, and lower part of another, both granite. Gunn MSS,XV.8; Notebook, IX, nos. 1, 2. Text of various fragments found in and around the tomb, id. ib. XIX, 39-42.

12. The mastaba of Khentika called Ikhekhi also has two false-door stelae in one room, both inscribed for the owner, see James and Apted, op. cit., 18.

13. W. M. F. Petrie, *The Arts and Crafts of Ancient Egypt* (Edinburgh and London, 1909), 69-74; 98-100.

14. The south temenos wall of the mastaba of Mereruka has also a rounded top. See Duell and others, op. cit., I, pl. 4A.

15. Firth and Gunn, op. cit., 27.

16. Duell and others, op. cit., I, pl. 4A.

17. James and Apted, op. cit., 18, 19, has also a temenos wall at the east side.

18. Note particularly the modelling of the leg as well as the arm muscles, and the representation of the breast and navel.

19. *iry-pꜥt*: On the reading and meaning of this title, see A.H. Gardiner, Ancient Egyptian Onomastica (London, 1947), I, 18* -19*.

20. *tꜣyty sꜣb ṯꜣty*: It has been suggested that, as several persons styled themselves *tꜣyty sꜣb ṯꜣty* at that time, this title was merely honorific. While there is no means of proving that Rēꜥ-wer acted as a vizier to Teti, the position of the tomb directly in front of the Mortuary Temple might suggest that he did so. See C. M. Firth and B. Gunn, Teti Pyramid Cemeteries, I, (Cairo, 1926), 109, n. 3.

21. *imꜣ-ꜥ* : This title, the meaning of which is obscure, must have been an important one, as it is found with several viziers of the Old Kingdom. See Kagemni (Firth and Gunn, op. cit., 105-6), Mereruka (ibid. 131), Tjetju (ibid., 152). For other important officials holding this title, see Seshemnefer, (IV) (H. Junker, Giza, III, 10), Biw (G. Jéquier, Le monument funéraire de Pepi II, II, pl. 57). See also Wb I, 81, where another reading, *bꜣḳ-ꜥ* (?), is given.

22. *smsw snwt* : Firth and Gunn, op. cit., 133.

23. *sm(t)* : (Semet-priest). The late form of this title is *stm*; early variants suggest that the original reading was *Smt* : see Gardiner, Onomastica, I, 39*; A-120.

24. *ꜥḏ-mr Dp* : Firth and Gunn, op. cit., I, 133 (for *ꜥḏ mr Dp* and *ꜥḏ-mr Dpiw*).

25. Note the modelling of the leg and arm muscles, breast and navel.

26. In this figure the arm holding the staff is attached to Rēꜥ-wer's right shoulder, and should therefore be his right arm. Yet the hand is turned so that its back is towards the observer, as if it were Rēꜥ-wer's left hand. Likewise, while the arm holding the sceptre is attached to the left shoulder, the fingers of the hand are clenched round the handle of the sceptre as though it were the right hand. These facts receive their explanation from the representation in the north jamb of the door, where the staff is shown held by the left hand, and the sceptre by the right. Both hands are there in the correct position. Thus it is clear that the sculptor intended that Rēꜥ-wer should carry the staff in the left hand and the sceptre in the right. But the necessity of showing Rēꜥ-wer striding out from his tomb on both jambs has meant that Rēꜥ-wer's right shoulder is inevitably in front on the south jamb. As the arm holding the staff was intended to be advanced, the sculptor has adopted the

device of attaching what is really Rēʿ-wer's left arm to his right shoulder, but showing that this is so by the position of the hand. In such instances the sculptor's procedure has clearly been carefully thought out. For a discussion, see W. Stevenson Smith, A history of Egyptian sculpture and painting in the Old Kingdom, (London, 1946), 274-8.

27. This damage, as on the north jamb, seems to be mainly in the area of the front of the kilt, though here there is also considerable damage to the upper torso. No clear difference in technique can be observed between this damage and that on the faces, except that on the kilt it is more sporadic and has the appearance of being less deliberate.

28. See note 26 on the south entrance door-jamb.

29. These inscriptions have been restored according to Gunn MSS, XIX, 37 (for the present reliefs see pl. 3, no. 2; pl. 20, no. 2). Gunn mentioned in his records that the *ḥwt* is coloured in red.

30. The *ḫpš*, foreleg; this seems to have been the most important joint of the sacrificial animal because of its symbolic importance in the ritual of the Opening of the Mouth. See W. Barta, Die altägyptische Opferliste (Berlin, 1963), 78-82.

31. The state of the text here is not easy to understand:

a. The title *sḏꜣwty-bỉty* has been written smaller than the remainder of the text, and has been crowded in. Yet there is no trace of any sign belonging to an earlier inscription at this point, nor of its defacement, so *sḏꜣwty-bỉty* can hardly be part of a usurpation.

b. The name of Rēʿ-wer has, as usual, been hammered out, and traces of the tail and feet of *wr* are still visible.

c. Dr. G. T. Martin has checked the false-door, and says that *sḏꜣwty-bỉty* is certainly part of the original titulary of Rēʿ-wer, and the surviving traces of the personal name show that the name was written (with the signs arranged thus to take account of the available space).

d. Elsewhere, the name of Rēʿ-wer was always inscribed in the false-doors in a vertical line, i.e. , not horizontally
It is written horizontally in incised hieroglyphs at the bottom of this vertical line, below *sḏꜣwty-bỉty*, not because it is a usurpation but because there is no room to write it in a vertical line. The title *sḏꜣwty-bỉty* also occurs on both jambs of the entrance to the tomb in the fourth of the seven lines, so was therefore always part of the owner's titulary and not a late addition to it.

32. G. Jéquier, Les frises d'objets (Cairo, 1921), 146; G. Maspero, La table d'offrandes (Paris, 1897), 344-5; Dümichen,"Ein salbölrecept aus dem Laboratorium des Edfutempels," ZÄS, 17, (1879), 100.

33. Maspero, op. cit., 343.

34. Ibid., 343. Jéquier, op. cit., 148. For another form of writing for this oil, see Wb II, 319. See also Junker, Giza, I, 108; II, 75; IV, 70; and Selim Hassan, Excavations at Giza (Cairo, 1948), VI, part II, 248-50.

35. Maspero, op. cit., 345; Jéquier, op. cit., 148.

36. Compare the other writing for the same oil on the north false-door (see pl. 8).

37. Compare the writing of this oil on the opposite jamb in the same false-door (pl. 8); and the same version on the northern false-door jamb, (pl. 4, no. 3).

38. See P. E. Newberry, Ancient Egypt (1915), 97-100.

39. In both places where the name is written, the signs, though only roughly scratched, are clear, except for that above . This may perhaps be the star , but it is far from certain. If the whole is a personal name, it does not appear to correspond exactly with any quoted in H. Ranke, Die ägyptischen Personennamen. 2 vols., (Glückstadt, Hamburg, 1935, 1952). It may, however, perhaps be analysed as the name *ỉpỉ* with a following description of his function, e.g. "of the door(?) of the lord", i.e. a doorkeeper. It seems likely to be one of those names which are found with the name of the obscure deity *ỉpỉ*, of *ỉpỉ-m-s3-f*, below p. 39).

40. It is not possible to make out here which way round Rēˁ-wer's hands are shown (see note 26 on the southern entrance door jamb).

41. The green-painted hieroglyphs end in the four jambs (E. G. F. H.) at *mry nṯr*. It will be observed that the titles inscribed below are in hieroglyphs which are slightly smaller and in a different technique. This may be observed in the photograph (pl. 21, no. 8) and the drawing (pl. 9).

42. : possibly *ḫt nbt*, "every thing" if the two *t*s have been left out; but this would seem exceptional following *n.f*. Perhaps *rˁ-nb* is preferable.

43. The *mr* sign is rather curiously positioned vis-à-vis the *nṯr* (see pl. 9; 21, no. 8). The signs *mry-nṯr* have been incised in a smaller hand over the original effaced inscription, clearly visible traces of which read *ḥ3ty-ˁ*.

44. In columns O.R the name *Rˁ-wr* has as usual been mutilated, leaving some traces in each case.

45. The signs *mry nṯr* have been inscribed in a smaller hand over the original effaced inscription, traces of which show that *sḏ3wty-bity* stood here.

46. The signs *mry nṯr* have been inscribed in a smaller hand, replacing an original effaced inscription, of which the surviving traces suggest the reading *smr wˁty*; but the latter title was written.

47. The signs *mry nṯr* are here inscribed in a smaller hand after *ṯȝyty sȝb ṯȝty*, replacing an original effaced inscription, of which the surviving traces suggest the reading *ḥȝty-ʿ*.

48. Gardiner, ZÄS, 42 (Leipzig, 1903-5), 15, line 1.

49. M. A. Murray, Saqqara Mastabas, I (London, 1905), 36. For the history of this sacred oil, see Selim Hassan, Excavation at Giza, VI, part 11, 241-43.

50. These inscriptions have been restored according to Gunn MSS,XIX,36. (For the present reliefs see pl. 10).

51. D. M. Dixon, Journal of Human Evolution I (1972), 441-4.

52. M. A. Murray, op. cit., pl. XXIII.

53. Seated headless statue of deceased, and lower part of another, both granite. Gunn MSS,XV,8; notebook IX, 1, 2.

54. "Left" and "right" from the point of view of the spectator, Gunn MSS XV, 8, 1.

55. The name  *Rʿ-wr* has here been intentionally erased, but it is still visible; Gunn MSS XV, 8, 2.

56. The sign *šmʿ*  (according to Gunn MSS IX, 1) is written the wrong way round.

57. For Akhpet, see Lauer and Leclant, op. cit., 7.

58. J. E. Quibell, Excavations at Saqqara, 1906-1907 (Cairo, 1908), 3.

59. *Ppi-ḥȝ-išṭf* : This name appears not to be attested in Ranke, op. cit., nor in the files of the Topographical Bibliography. Compare *'Ipi-ḥȝ-iš-wt.f*, Ranke, op. cit. II, 262, no. 28. And *Tty-išt.f*, Ranke, op. cit. I, 384, note 12, II, 330, no. 16.

60.  is exceptional. (Wb. III, 394).

61. Ranke: op. cit., I, 22, no. 17.

62. The final group  *r* may be the beginning of the owner's name, or part of a second title (e.g. 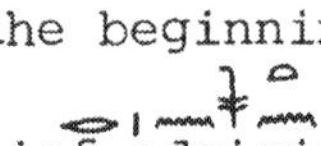 *r n nsw*, "mouth of the king"; or 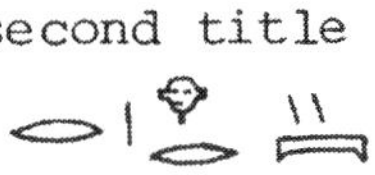 *r ḥry* "Chief administrator", Wb. II, 390, 1; 6-9).

63. For *ȝbd* as a personal name, see H. Ranke, op. cit. I, 28, 2, no. 2, 4.

64. '*Ini* : See Ranke, op. cit. I, 32, no. 19. Used by both male and female in the Middle Kingdom. Compare no. 21.

65. In view of the frequent occurence of *sš-nsw mȝʿ* the *ṯ* is probably a scribal error, as also perhaps is the  *n* before *sš-nsw*.

66. James and Apted, op. cit. 13.

67. P. Duell, and others, op. cit. I, pls. 79, 81.

68. PM III, 2nd ed. Pt. 1 (Oxford, 1977), 558.

69. See note 20 (on *tꜣyty sꜣb ṯꜣty*).

70. *Mḥw* : Saad, ASAE 40 (1941), 687-90; Hussein, ASAE 42 (1943), 417-25, pls. 29-38. *Mrri* : Selim Hassan, Saqqara 3, 25 ff. *Mrri-Tti*, son of *Mrrw-kꜣ* Daressy, Le mastaba de Mera, MIE 3, 521-74. *Idw-nfr* : Junker, Giza 8, 66-90. *Ṯtw* : Firth-Gunn, Teti pyramid cemeteries I, 28-31, 151-56; II, pls. 38, 51, 61. *Rʿ-wr*.

71. Sethe, Urkunden I, 209 ff; Goedicke, Königliche Dokumente, 55 ff., fig. 5.

72. The names are written on the Decree without name determinatives, which are always present in the tomb. See note 70 above.

73. Erased titles both precede and follow *nsw*.

74. Goedicke, op. cit., 57, (3). Sethe restores simply *sš nsw*.

75. See above p. 26.

76. See above p. 45.

INDEXES

1. Deities

2. Royal Names

3. Personal Names

4. Geographical Names

5. Titles of Rēꜥ-wer

6. Other Titles

7. Egyptian Words

PLATES

PLATE 1

PLATE 2

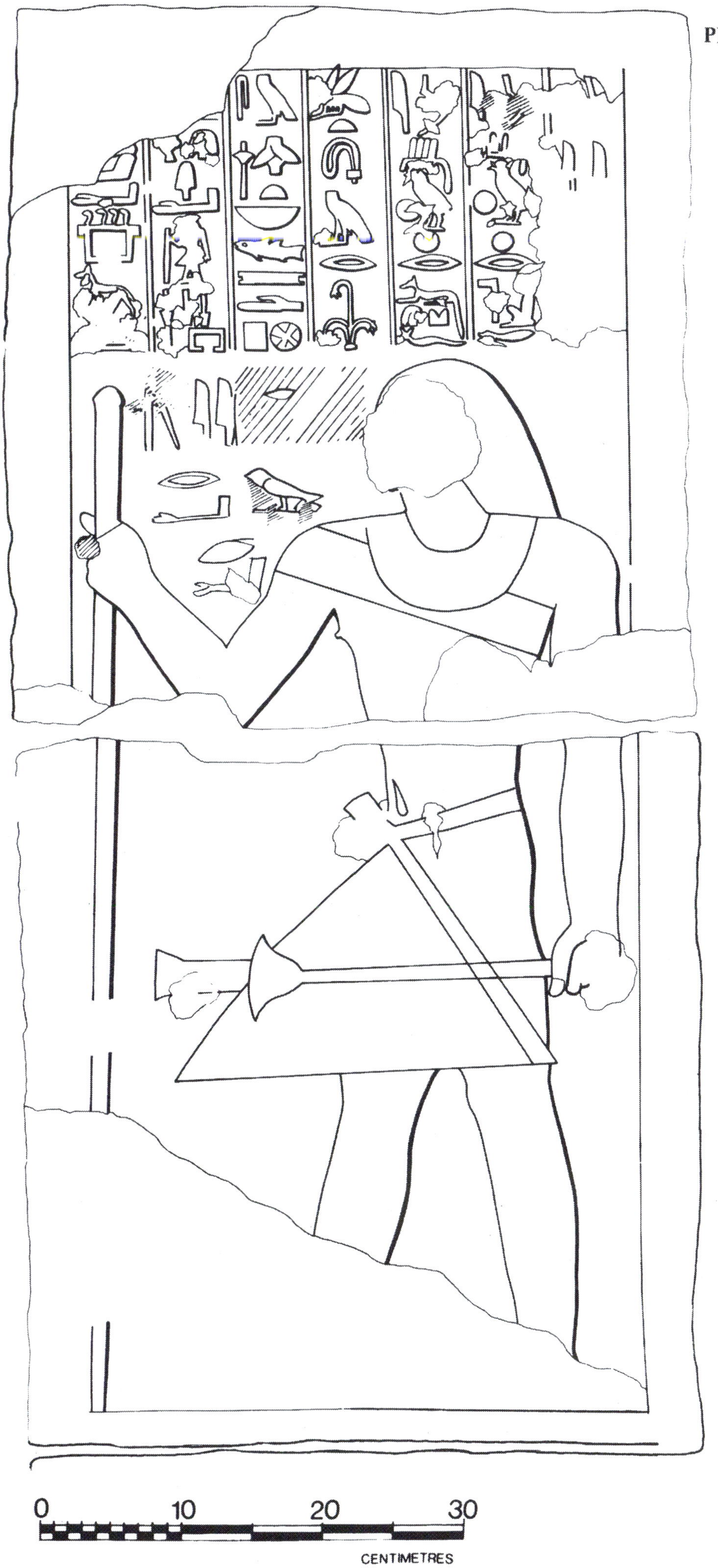

PLATE 3

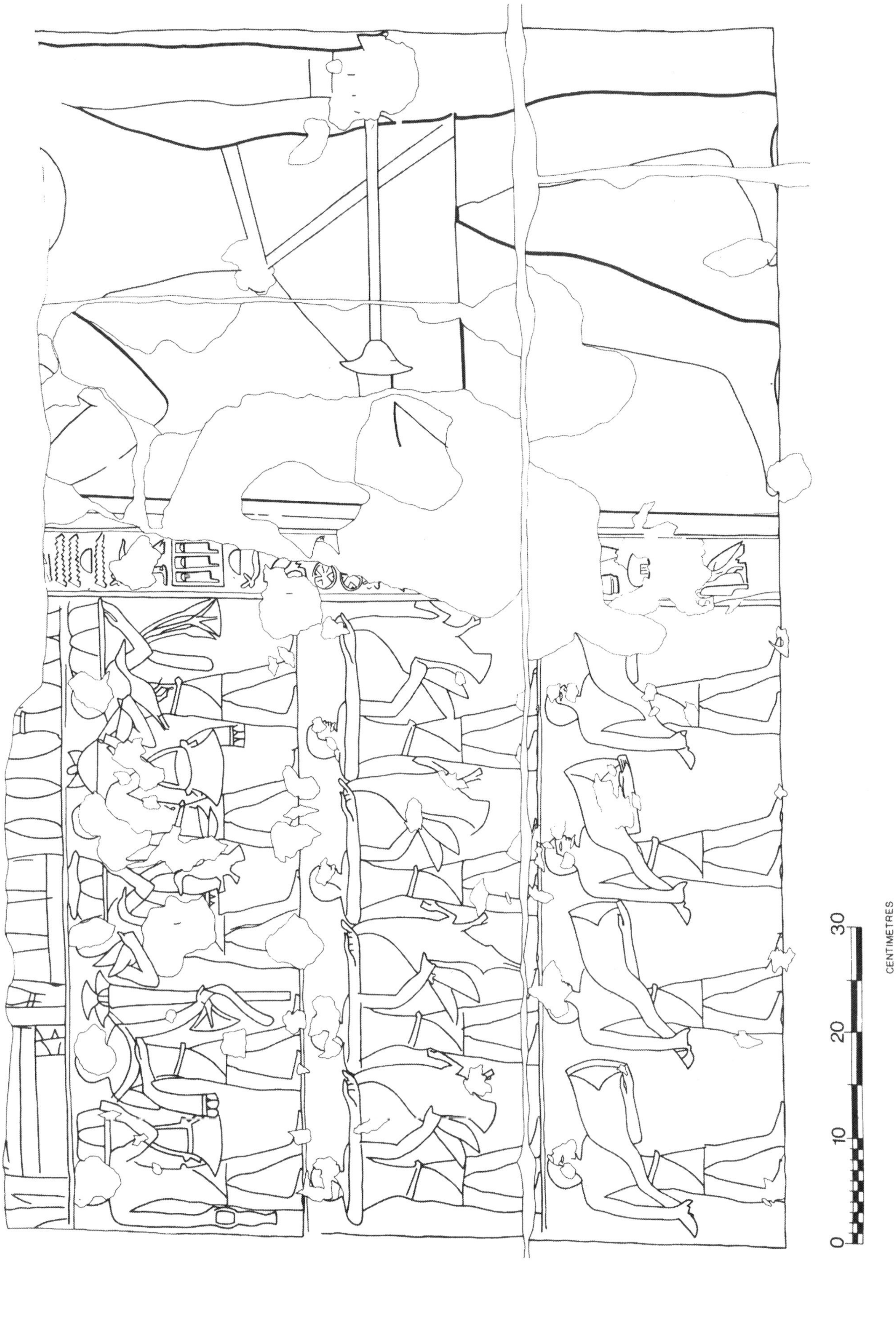

3

5

PLATE 5

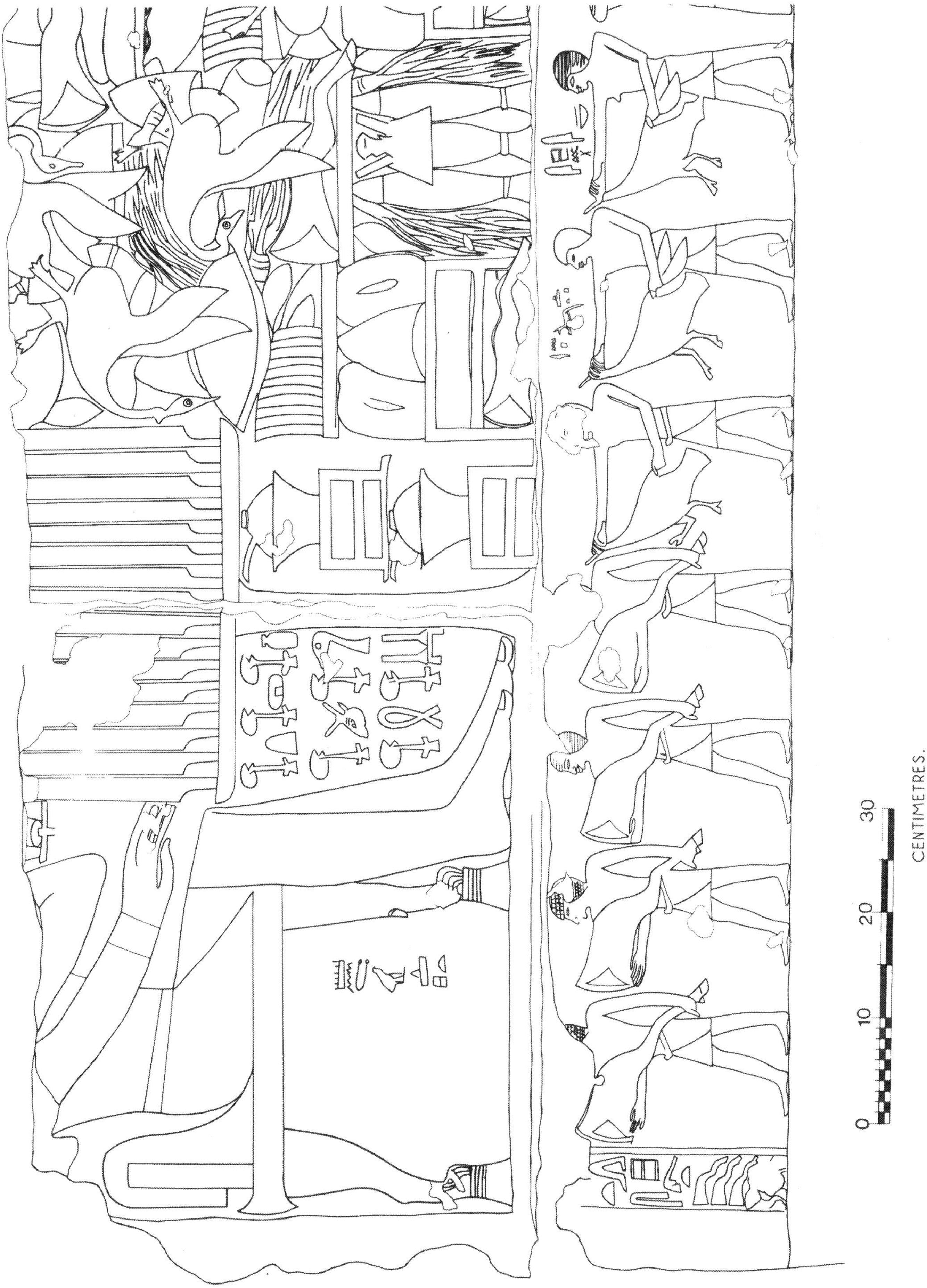
0
10
20
30
CENTIMETRES.

PLATE 7

7

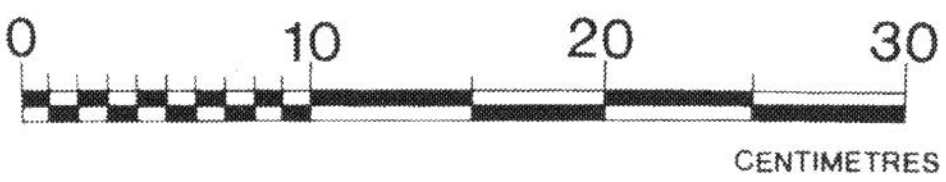

9

PLATE 9

PLATE 10

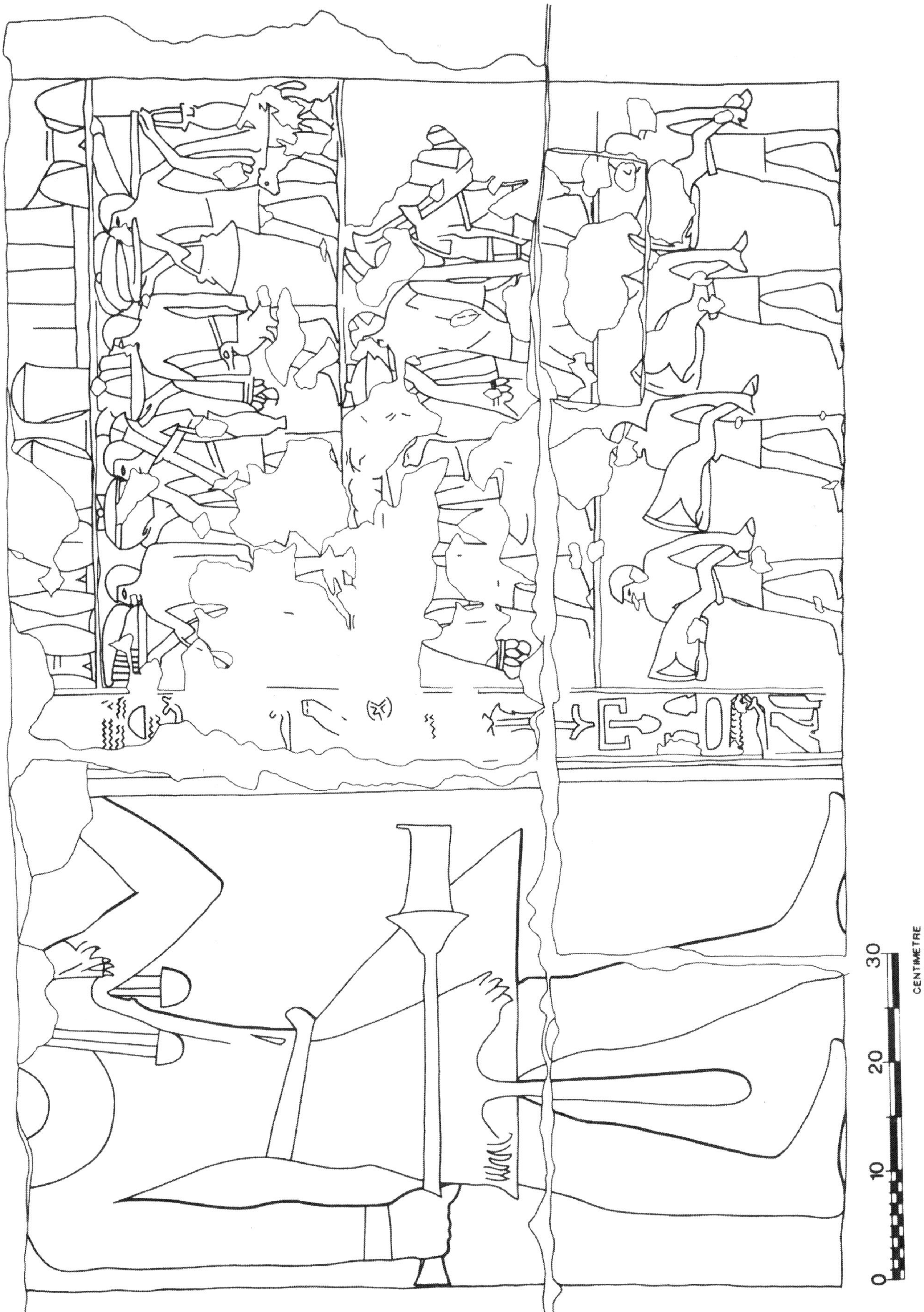

PLATE 11

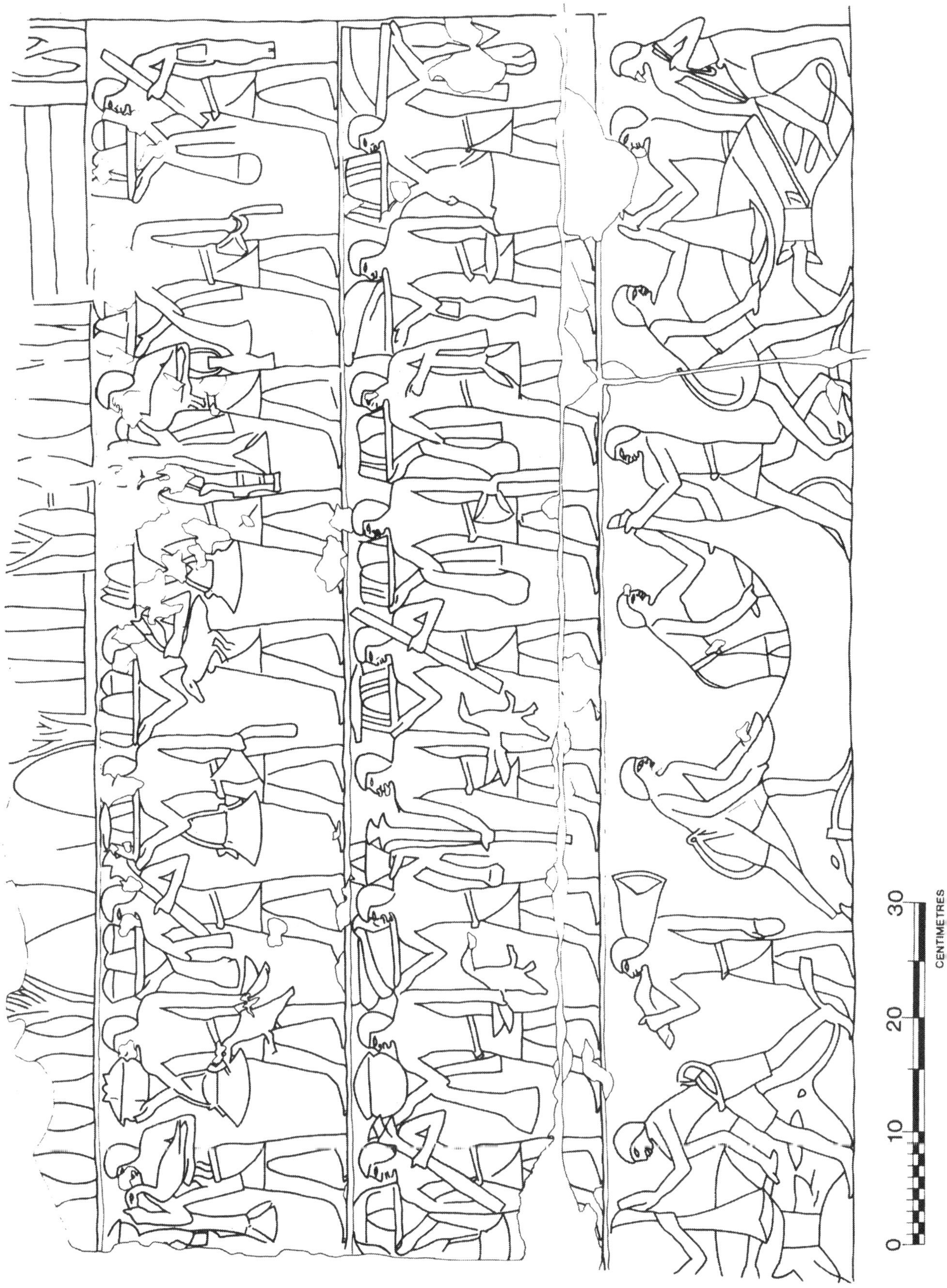

PLATE 12

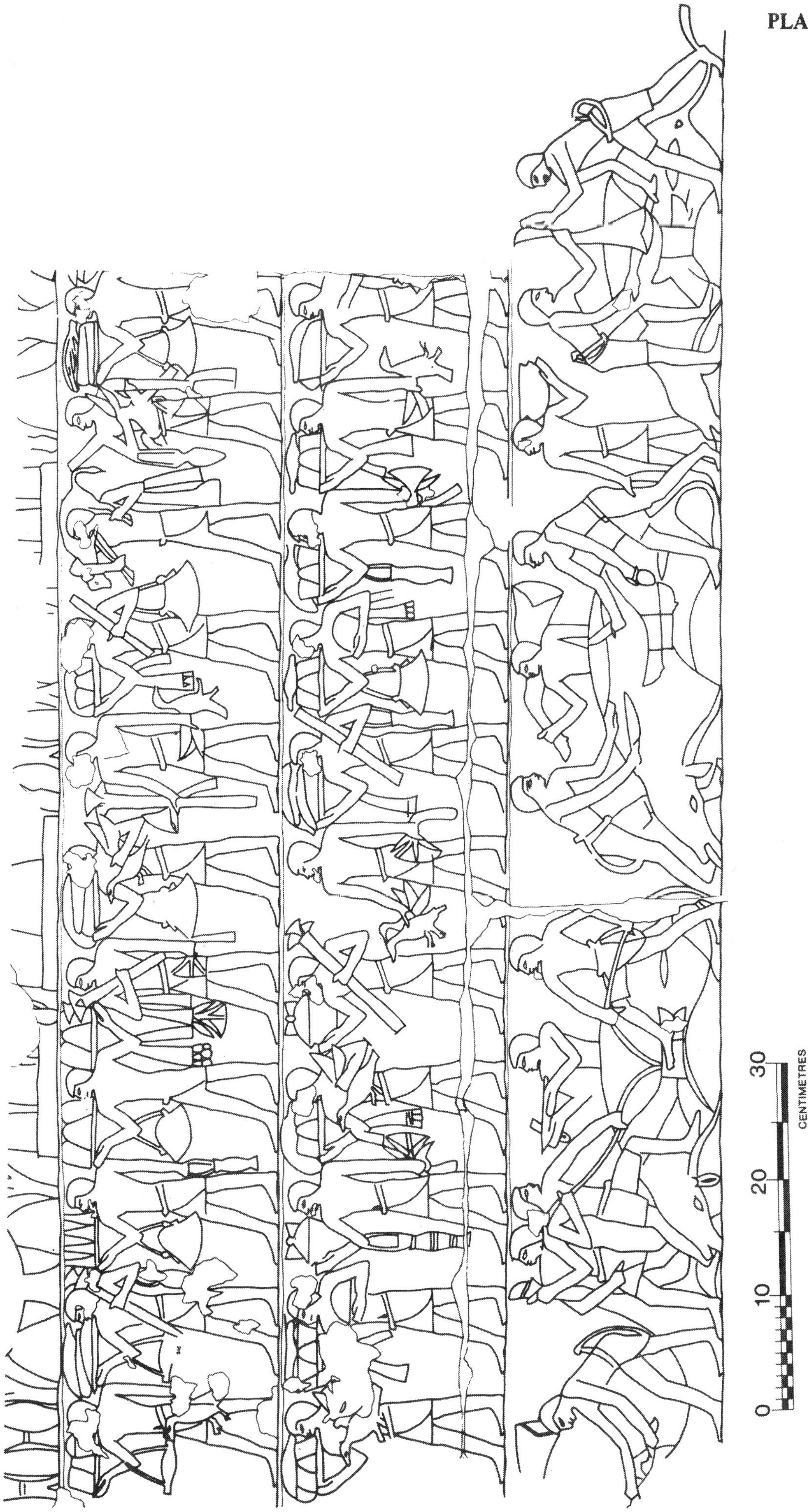

PLATE 13

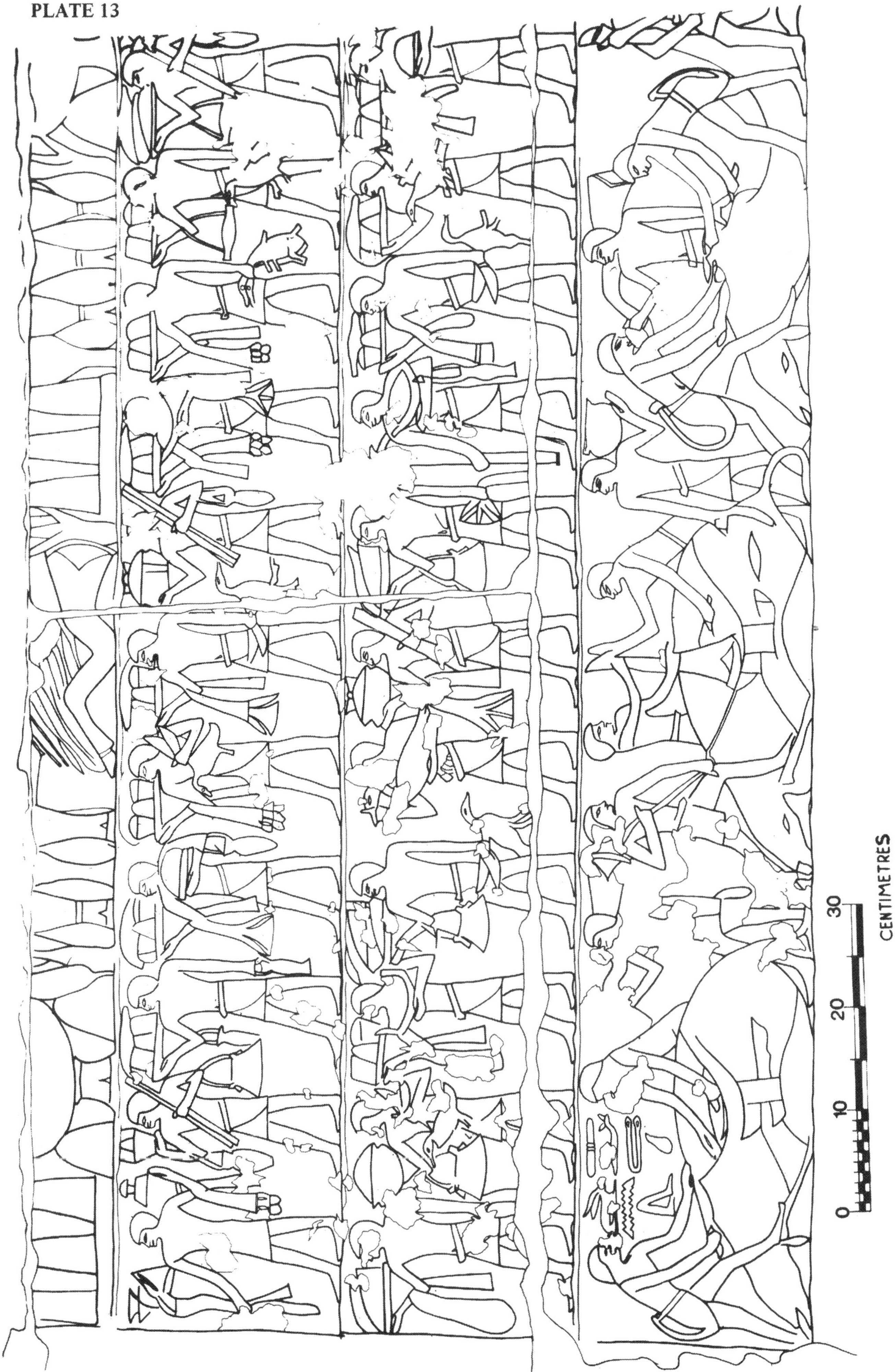

PLATE 14

PLATE 15

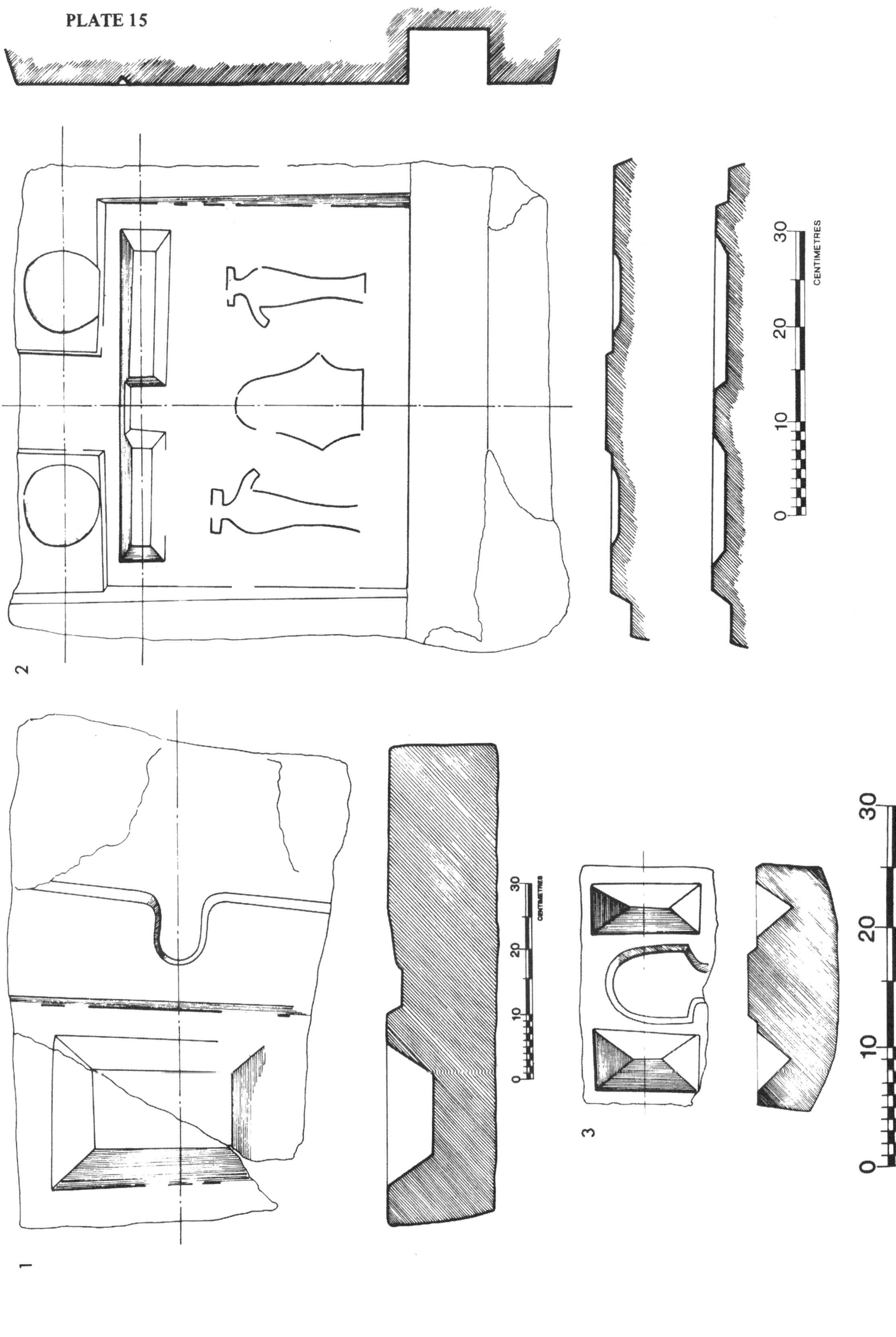

5

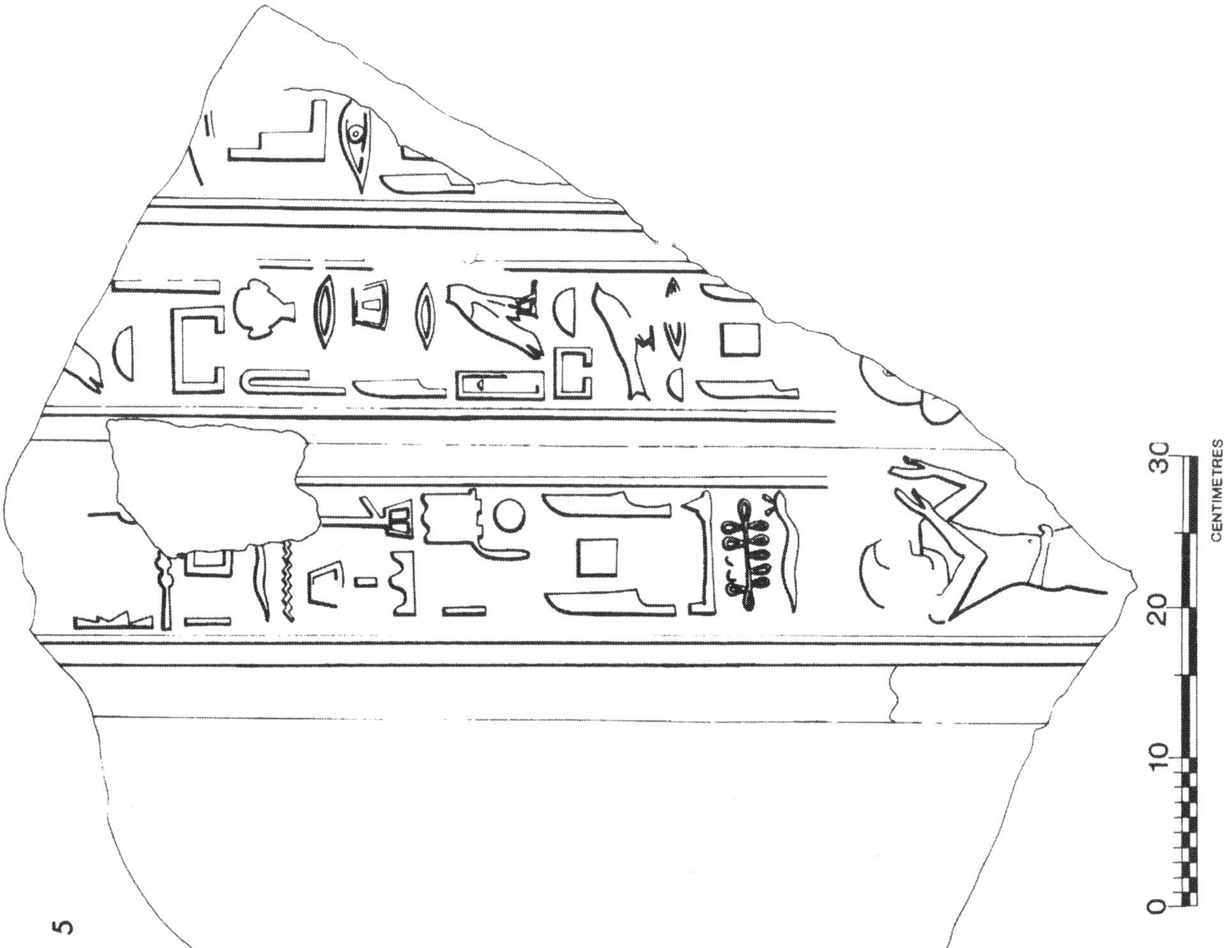

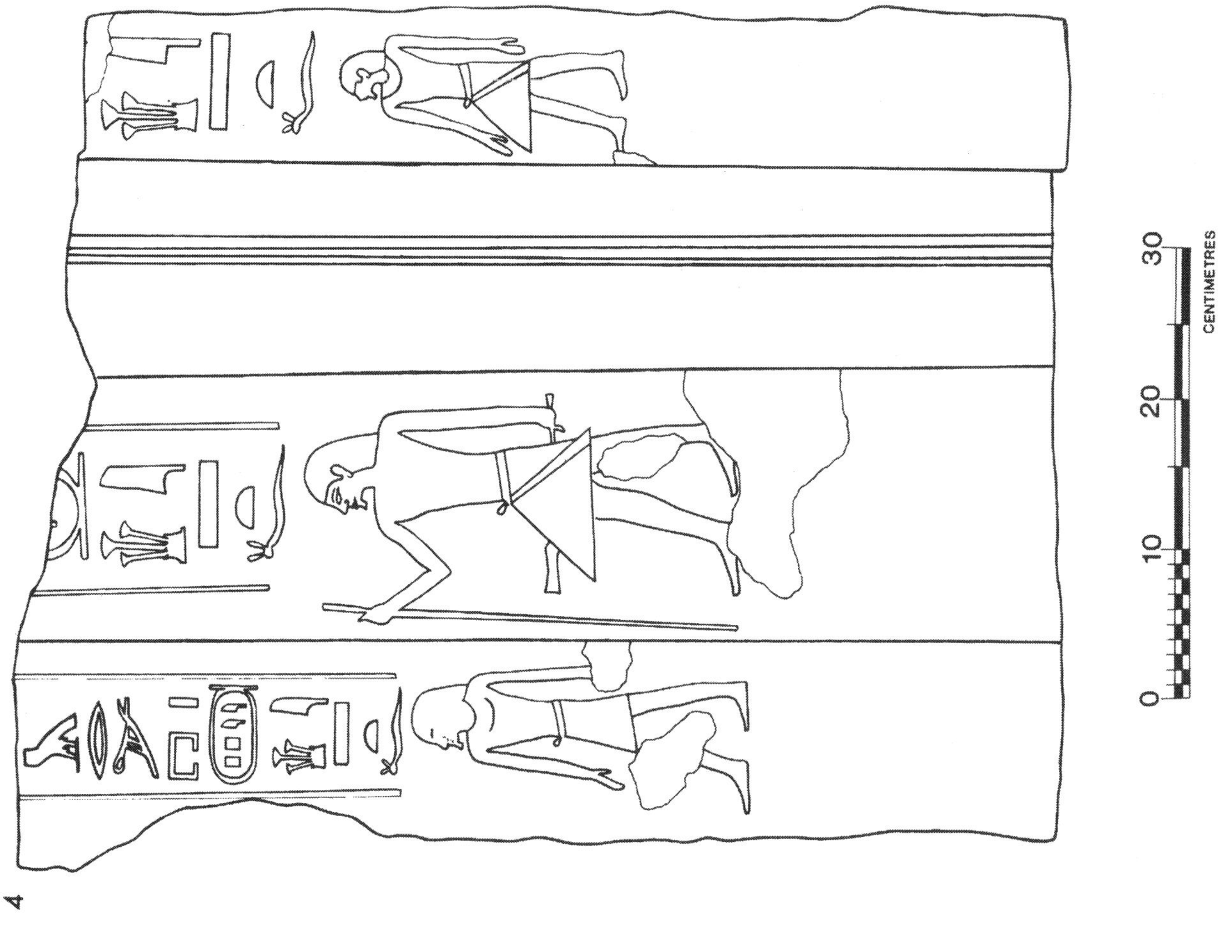

4

PLATE 17

6

7

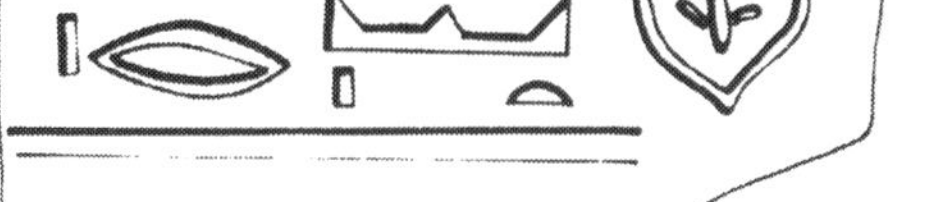

a

2

b

c

1

PLATE 19

A

A

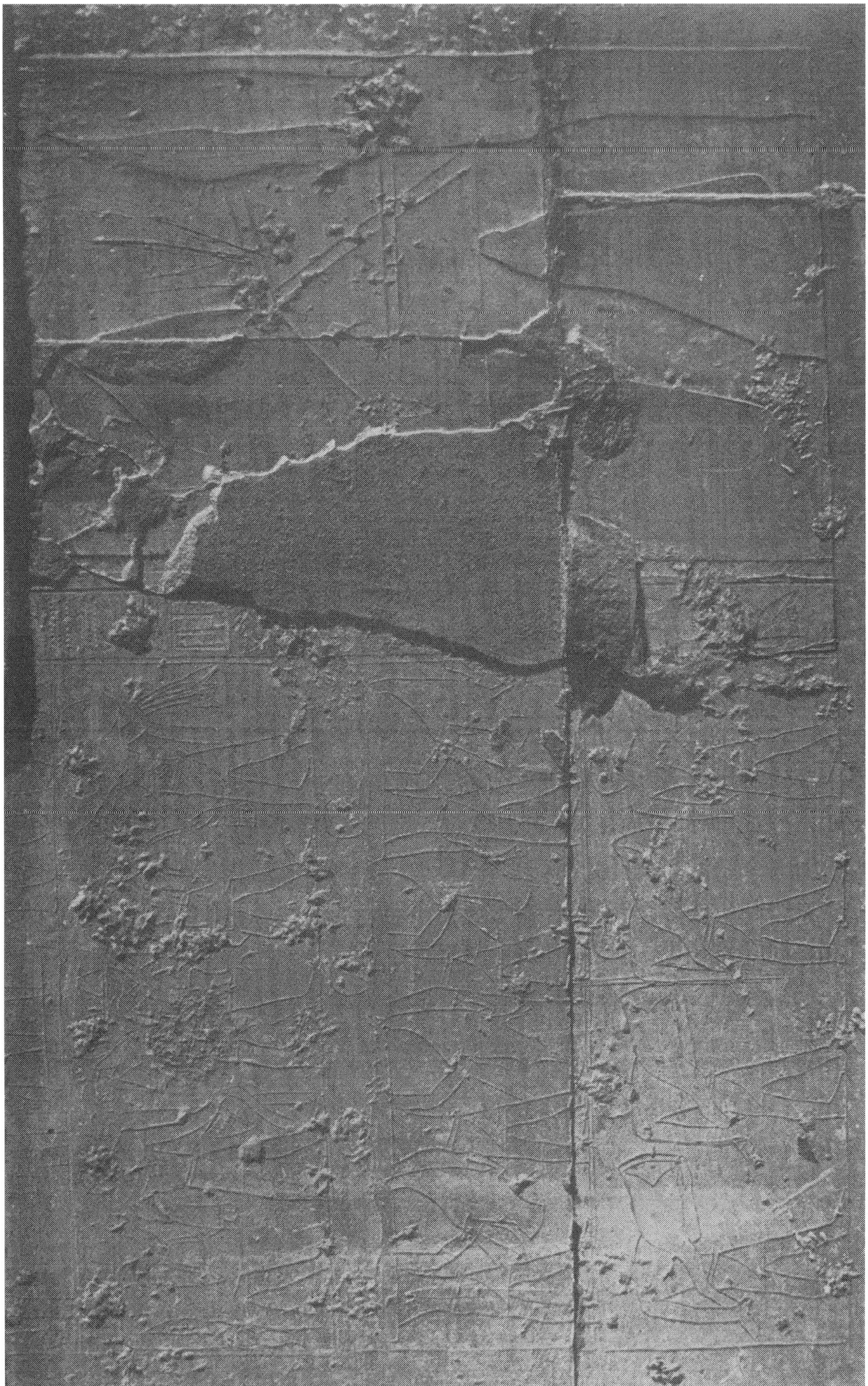

B

8

4